Made for Love, Loved by God

FR. PETER JOHN CAMERON, O.P.

SERVANT
BOOKS

PUBLISHED BY FRANCISCAN MEDIA
Cincinnati, Ohio

Unless otherwise noted, Scripture passages have been taken from the *Revised Standard Version*, Catholic edition. Copyright 1946, 1952, 1971 by the Division of Christian Education of the National Council of Churches of Christ in the USA. Used by permission. All rights reserved. Quotations are taken from the English translation of the *Catechism of the Catholic Church* for the United States of America (indicated as CCC), 2nd ed. Copyright 1997 by United States Catholic Conference—Libreria Editrice Vaticana.

Cover design by Candle Light Studio
Cover image: Christ at the Pool of Bethesda | Murillo, Bartolome Esteban (1618-82 | National Gallery, London, UK | The Bridgeman Art Library
Book design by Mark Sullivan

LIBRARY OF CONGRESS CATALOGING-IN-PUBLICATION DATA
Cameron, Peter John, O.P.
Made for love, loved by God / by Fr. Peter John Cameron, O.P.
pages cm
Includes bibliographical references.
ISBN 978-1-61636-635-3 (alk. paper)
1. God (Christianity)—Love. 2. Love—Religious aspects—Christianity.
3. Catholic Church—Doctrines. I. Title.
BT140.C25 2014
231'.6—dc23
2014002138

ISBN 978-1-61636-635-3

Published by Servant Books, an imprint of Franciscan Media
28 W. Liberty St.
Cincinnati, OH 45202
www.FranciscanMedia.org

Printed in the United States of America.
Printed on acid-free paper.
14 15 16 17 18 5 4 3 2 1

For my friend
Fr. Harry Cornelius Cronin, C.S.C.,
in honor of his Golden Jubilee of Ordination
to the Priesthood

Your merciful love is better than life.
—PSALM 63:3

The LORD takes pleasure...
in those who hope in his steadfast love.
—PSALM 147:11

The human being lives on truth and on being loved: on
being loved by the truth. He needs God, the God who
draws close to him, interprets for him the meaning of life,
and thus points him toward the path of life.[1]
—POPE BENEDICT XVI

Everything is for giving away.[2]
—WILLIAM PERALDUS, O.P. (+1271)

Lord, help me to love you the way that you love me.

CONTENTS

CHAPTER ONE

HUNGER FOR LOVE

Then the Divine Goodness, regarding with the eye of His mercy the hunger and desire of that soul, said:...

"The soul cannot live without love, but always wants to love something, because she is made of love, and, by love, I created her.... The affection moved the intellect, saying, as it were, 'I will love, because the food on which I feed is love.'"[3]

—ST. CATHERINE OF SIENA

"I love you." Who would ever dare to live life without those words?

Jean Vanier (born 1928) is the founder of *L'Arche,* an international federation of group homes both for people with developmental disabilities and for those who assist them. Several years ago I remember being struck by a passage in one of his books. It was about an eight-year-old boy named Armando:

Armando cannot walk or talk and is very small for his age. He came to us from an orphanage where he had been abandoned. He no longer wanted to eat because he no longer wanted to live cast off from his mother. He was desperately thin and was dying of lack of food. After a while in our community where he found people who held him, loved him and wanted him to live, he gradually began to eat again and to develop in a remarkable way. He still cannot walk or talk or eat by himself, his body is twisted and broken, and he has a severe mental disability, but when you pick him up, his eyes and his whole body quiver with joy and excitement and say: "I love you." He has a deep therapeutic influence on people.[4]

In some ways we are all like Armando. Despite our loneliness, our powerlessness, our brokenness, something drives us and refuses to die. We are a hunger for love. And when at last that love comes and finds us, picks us up and holds us close, it transforms us. We become love for others.

This is why Jesus commands, "Unless you turn and become like children, you will never enter the kingdom of heaven" (Matthew 18:3). The total receptivity to love modeled by that defenseless young boy is what equips us best for heaven.

THE HUMAN NEED FOR LOVE

To be human is to *be* need. To be human is to be need *for love*. "What we need over and above sheer existence," wrote the Catholic theologian Josef Pieper (+1997) "is to be loved by another person. Being created by God actually does not suffice, it would seem; the fact of creation needs continuation and perfection by the creative power of human love."[5]

A few years ago a friend of mine was enjoying a visit one evening from his preschool granddaughter. They stood stargazing in the backyard when, to their delight, a shooting star streaked across the sky. Both immediately made a wish. The little girl wanted to share hers.

"Grandpa," she said, "I wished that you would love me forever."

Gasp. The child did not know that that love was hers already. Nor did she take it for granted. She didn't wish for toys, or riches, or the joys only a child's mind can imagine. Rather, her tiny heart told her that she needed her grandfather's love more than anything else in the world. So she dared to expend a rare and priceless wish to keep that love from ending.

It's the promise of such a love that makes us get out of bed in the morning and gives us the courage to face the next five minutes.

In the early 1990s I was assigned to an apostolate in Los Angeles, California. It was a time when crime committed by street gangs there reached crisis proportions. Social scientists conducted studies to get at what was behind it all. Why did young people join street gangs? Was it for the thrill of violence? For the chance to wreak mayhem? To rebel against the establishment? To indulge in drugs and dereliction?

The findings indicated no—it was none of those things. What drew teenagers to gangs was simply the desire to *belong*. Fragmented families, absent or abusive parents, left many youth feeling alienated, anxious, and alone. The isolation was too much for them. Better to opt for membership in a gang—as perilous and deviant as that choice was—than to endure the unbearable pain of belonging to no one.

I grew up in a suburb with parents who loved me. Yet even with that assurance, I was always looking for more love. The high point of my little-boy life was getting a visit from my Italian grandparents, who lived in a neighboring state. Noni and Nono we called them.

My brothers and I would stand out on the cement front steps of our yellow house laser-beaming Hany Lane with our eyes, willing Nono's car to materialize. Yes, they came laden with chocolate-frosted doughnuts and rigatoni in Noni's homemade, to-die-for spaghetti sauce. But it was more than that. I would burst in expectation of their arrival because I felt loved by them like nothing else in the world.

As I grew into my jaded teenage years, even their love seemed to be not enough. The need in me became a wound. Then one evening in 1974, I sat with my siblings watching a made-for-TV movie called *Bad Ronald* (which I would recommend to no one).

The premise of the film is this:

Ronald Wilby is a sweet but nerdy only child who lives alone in a big, old house with his divorced, neurotic, overprotective mother. His estranged father wants nothing to do with them. Ronald is preoccupied with preparing for college as a premed major, with composing and illustrating science fiction fantasy stories, and with Laurie Matthews, the neighborhood blonde-haired beauty of his dreams.

On Ronald's seventeenth birthday, he gets dressed up and takes himself over to Laurie's house, where she and her friends are frolicking in the family pool. When Ronald presents himself poolside in the hopes of spending some time alone with Laurie, the gang of them go at him. They taunt and ridicule Ronald, mock him mercilessly for his crush on Laurie, splash him with water. But the cruelest of them all is Laurie herself who finds Ronald's pining for her repugnant. She reacts with searing meanness, rejecting him. She practically *blames* Ronald for his tender feelings, turning his heartfelt affection into an offense.

Spurned and dejected, Ronald leaves, taking a shortcut through the hedges. Whereupon he collides with Carole, Laurie's younger sister, who is out riding her bike. And despite being half Ronald's age, Carole proceeds to bully and berate him, spewing insulting things about both Ronald and his mother. He pushes the girl to the ground. She hits her head and dies.

The panic-stricken Ronald confesses to his mother. Desperate to keep her son from prison, Mrs. Wilby devises a macabre plan: they will plaster over the door of a bathroom, and Ronald will live there, hidden from the world in this ingenious secret chamber.

But...Mrs. Wilby then dies—unbeknownst to Ronald—and he is left to languish within the walls of the house alone. Of course, the plot takes some offbeat twists from there. But the point is: When the movie was over, I was a wreck. Why? Because I felt like it was all about me. And I was stunned that my brothers and sisters didn't feel the same.

That pathetic story got me asking: *Is this what happens when you dare to pursue the need to be loved—that all the world turns on you with derision and abuse and contempt? So what if I am awkward, and socially inept, and even a dweeb? Does that mean that I'm disqualified from love? That there's no love out there for me? Is this what listening to your heart and taking a risk does: make you crazed and violent and dangerous? Turn you into someone on the run? Make you a captive? Wall you up in your own overwhelming emotion? Abandon you to an even worse loneliness? If that is so, then the hunger for love is a curse!*

I could identify entirely with the wretched Ronald Wilby. How ironic the way he resembled the innocent victim murdered for no reason in Edgar Allan Poe's disturbing short story "The Tell-Tale Heart." From its place under the floorboards where he had buried the victim's corpse, the hateful killer still could hear "the beating of his hideous heart."

Nothing can silence that heart.

Our need for love cannot be killed. Look at the Samaritan woman at the well (John 4:4–42). She had had five husbands, and the man she is living with when we meet her is not her husband. Not one of the men has been enough for her heart. All the same, she does not give up on love, because she has a hunger for love. Or maybe in her case it would be better to say that she has a *thirst* for love. For in order to woo the woman to what will truly satisfy the infinite longing of her heart, Jesus says, "If you knew the gift of God, and who it is that is saying to you, 'Give me a drink,' you would have asked him and he would have given you living water" (John 4:11).

WHAT IS LOVE?

Hands down *the* most disturbing play that I have ever seen was a 2002 performance of the Broadway production of Edward Albee's *The Goat, or Who Is Sylvia?* (I sincerely hope that that play will never be produced again. The premise of it is so warped I almost don't want to tell you.)

The main character, Martin Gray, is a world-renowned, stupendously successful, award-winning architect who has everything any man could ever want: a beautiful wife, a devoted son, a perfect home, a world-class education, friends, affluence, power, leisure, approbation, privilege, fame, cachet—an idyllic existence. But for him it's not enough. One day while driving in the country, Martin stops at a farm to buy some vegetables. He sees a goat (Sylvia) looking at him, and he "falls in love."

The bulk of this tedious, Tony Award–winning play involves Martin revealing his six-month bout of bestiality to his friend, his wife, and his son. When the three rightly demand an explanation of how such a perverse thing could possibly be so, Martin returns the lamest replies: The goat was there, looking at him with "those eyes." He had never seen such an expression—so pure and trusting and innocent and guileless; when the goat looked at him with those eyes of hers, he melted.

To sit through the performance was nauseating (the decadence of the play is *far* worse than what I am describing), and I couldn't wait for it to be over. I understand why Albee wrote the thing in one act, because he must have sensed that if he inserted an intermission, decent people would flee. When it ended, I felt enraged at being held hostage by such depravity, deprived of any polite means of escape (I was sitting in the front row!).

I want to be open-minded, though. So, as revolting as it is, let's for a moment grant Martin Gray's heinous claim about the goat: "I love her and she loves me." For us to comprehend such a deviant idea, all we need is a simple statement *somewhere* in the play of what Martin/Albee means by *love*. But not a single hint is given. All *The Goat* offers about what justifies such a "love" are the vapid, insipid stupidities stated above. We are supposed to condone Martin's obsceneness because the goat has nice eyes? Really?

The truest judgment in the play is spoken by Martin's devastated wife: "How can you love me when you love so much less?" Martin can answer only with a tautology: "I *love* you. And I love *her*."

Although my disgust over this play has not lessened, now, ten years later, I see something deeper about it: The play is prophetic. It offers an invaluable commentary on our society. Ask almost anyone today what *love* is, what will they say? *Love is what makes me "feel good." I can love in any way I want as long as it doesn't hurt anybody.*

The reprehensible Martin Gray has become a hero of our modern, degenerate culture. But not for me. If I had the chance to have a conversation with Edward Albee, I would say to him: "Just be honest—because your play is not honest. What is Martin Gray really looking for in that goat? Or do you truly believe that the thing driving the insatiable heart of Martin Gray can actually be answered by an animal—or by any creature, for that matter?"

The one sublimely amazing thing about the play—once you get past its unrelenting repulsiveness—is that Martin-the-man-who-has-everything knows that he needs something more, and what he needs is *love*—a love beyond anything he has ever imagined. (Maybe this is why Albee gives the play the subtitle "Notes toward a definition of tragedy.") The hunger for love haunts us.

The main character of Flannery O'Connor's short story "Good Country People" is Joy Hopewell. Thirty-two years old with a PH.D. in philosophy, Joy is a self-professed atheist seething with issues and resentment. She brands herself "one of those people who see through to nothing." A large, spectacled, hulking woman who lives with her mother, Joy is always angry. Her "constant outrage had obliterated every expression from her face," as if she were "someone who has achieved blindness by an act of will and means to keep it."[6]

The source of all this hostility is a hunting accident dating from when Joy was a girl. Her leg had been shot off. Added to that is a serious heart condition, saddling Joy with a life expectancy of forty-five. She has managed to get by for more than twenty years with an artificial leg, ugly remarks, and a perpetually glum face.

Her revenge on a world that has robbed her of so much joy is a symbolic act of spite: She legally changes her name from Joy to Hulga, because she deems it "the ugliest name in any language." Bitterness turns Joy/Hulga supremely antisocial, especially when it comes to romance: "She looked at nice young men as if she could smell their stupidity."

But one day a young Bible salesman stops by the Hopewell house peddling his wares, and Mrs. Hopewell invites him to stay for dinner. The young man, Manley Pointer, catches Hulga's eye. After dinner she lingers outside on the road, waiting for the young man to come out of the house, and when he does the two talk briefly in secret. They plan a rendezvous.

The next morning Hulga makes her way to the gate per their arrangement. The boy greets her, and Manley and Hulga then walk together into the pasture toward the woods. Emerging on a sunlit hillside, they see the rusted roof of the old, two-story storage barn beyond the back fields, and they head for it. Upon reaching the barn, Hulga lumbers up the ladder to the hayloft. The young man follows, oddly toting his big, black valise full of Bibles. There he recommences his kisses, professes his love, and insists that Hulga do the same. When at last she does, the man demands proof of her love—to wit: He wants her to show him where her wooden leg joins on.

Hulga shudders with repulsion at such an obscene request, but Manley's "innocence" wins her over, and she concedes. "It was like surrendering to him completely. It was like losing her own life and finding it again, miraculously, in his."[7]

But things are not as they seem. The young man persuades Hulga to leave the leg off as he proceeds with further kisses and the suggestion of more sordid intimacy. Manley Pointer is not "good country people": He is a complete and total fraud, a cad, the name a fiction.

Hulga panics. She screams for the man to reattach her leg. Instead he grabs the leg, tosses it in his suitcase, slams the lid, and scurries down the ladder, out the barn, and across the fields to the highway, never to be seen again.

Joy/Hulga is left stranded and totally helpless. But there is a grace in this betrayal, in this risk she takes with love. For now her only recourse to be rescued from her predicament is to receive the charity of another. In her powerlessness and abandonment, Joy/Hulga has become like eight-year-old Armando. Surrendering herself completely to love, anatomically losing her own life, Joy discovers that life is about finding life in another's love. Her blindness is ended.

Sometimes we need to have our legs taken out from under us in order to accept our hunger for love.

THE KIND OF LOVE WE NEED

And not just any old love will do. Take the Gospel story of the rich young man. His legendary encounter with Jesus is recounted in the three synoptic Gospels—Matthew, Mark, and Luke—with variations (based on each evangelist's particular theological perspective). In Matthew (Matthew 19:16–30) he is young; in Mark (Mark 10:17–31) he is rich; and in Luke (Luke 18:18–30) he is a ruler. But we commonly blend them together to speak of the rich young ruler.

This fellow's privileged status gives him unlimited access to the four principal things people regularly resort to in attempts to fill the emptiness in their lives. The problem is that that aching void in us can be filled only by God. And the human heart deep down knows this.

Since the man is rich, he can purchase all the *possessions* he could ever want. Inasmuch as he is a young man, he is privy to any of the world's lush, abundant *pleasures*. And as a ruler he enjoys the benefits of plenteous *power* and *prestige*, with all their attendant celebrity, fame, clout, and acclaim.

But here's the thing: *These four p's were not enough for him!* And what's the proof? The man comes in search of *Jesus*. Despite all that is his—despite the advantage of unbridled luxury, indulgence, influence, and affluence—the rich young ruler is looking for Something More. He wants Jesus Christ.

The man asks, "Good Teacher, what must I do to inherit eternal life?" (Mark 10:17). Mark the evangelist makes a striking observation: "And Jesus looking upon him loved him, and said..." (Mark 10:21). And we know the rest of the sad story: "At that saying his countenance fell, and he went away sorrowful; for he had great possessions" (Mark 10:22).

But *is* that the end of the story? Mark also relates a famously perplexing detail in his Gospel about a young man who follows Jesus to Gethsemane dressed in nothing but a linen cloth. The young man runs away naked when the crowd tries to seize him with Jesus (Mark 14:51–52). Maybe *this* was the rich young ruler who permitted that look of love from Jesus to sink in, pierce his resistance, and melt his hard heart. Maybe he finally let himself be seized by Jesus's love.

For who has ever looked at us the way that this man looks at us? Jesus's look of love cuts through all our self-absorption and defenses, all our excuses, all our distractions and fixations, all our preconceptions and misgivings and guilt and fear, and penetrates to our truest *desire*.

The rich, young ruler found in the loving gaze Jesus what truly and completely corresponds with his heart.

The force of Christ's gaze constantly makes itself felt no matter how much we may try to defy it or rebel against it. Think of Peter after he betrayed Jesus three times at the fire. The very second after the cock crowed, "the Lord turned and looked at Peter" (Luke 22:61). That look of love turned Peter's cowardice into contrition; from it flowed a flood of repentant tears. Maybe it was just that look of love that saved Peter from becoming another despairing, suicidal Judas Iscariot.

THE CRY OF THE HEART

One somewhat notorious example involves the pitiful story of Madalyn Murray O'Hair. In 1963 the United States Supreme Court outlawed prayer in America's public schools. One of the plaintiffs in that case was America's best-known and most visible atheist, Madalyn Murray O'Hair. Over the years, O'Hair kept up an aggressive and even hostile campaign against religion in public life (she even had a plan to humiliate Rev. Billy Graham publicly on television).

Then one day O'Hair vanished, leaving her sports car in an airport parking lot and a half-million dollars missing from the American Atheists bank account. Her disappearance remains an unsolved mystery.

The Internal Revenue Service seized O'Hair's home to pay her creditors and back taxes. Her personal effects were auctioned off, and among the items was her diary. One diary entry reads, "The whole idiotic hopelessness of human relations descends upon me. Tonight, I cried and cried, but even then feeling nothing."[8] But what hits hardest are four words repeated by O'Hair in the diary at least half a dozen times: "Somebody, somewhere, love me."[9]

Those words are what we call *prayer*. They are a plaintive cry of the human heart to the Maker of the human heart begging for the only thing that will satisfy the human heart: God's love given as a gift.

One could easily mistake Madalyn Murray O'Hair's anguished plea with entreaties dotting the book of Psalms:

> As a deer longs
>   for flowing streams,
> so longs my soul
>   for you, O God.
> My soul thirsts for God,
>   for the living God.
> When shall I come and behold
>   the face of God? (Psalm 42:1–2)

> O God, you are my God, I seek you,
>   my soul thirsts for you;
> my flesh faints for you,
>   as in a dry and weary land where no water is.
>   ...
> [Y]our merciful love is better than life. (Psalm 63:1, 3)

> [The LORD] heals the brokenhearted,
>   and binds up their wounds....
>   his understanding is beyond measure.
> The LORD lifts up the downtrodden....
> The LORD takes pleasure...
>   in those who hope in his steadfast love. (Psalm 147:3, 5b–6a, 11)

Or these words from the Song of Songs:

> Arise, my love, my fair one,
>   ...
> let me see your face,
>   let me hear your voice,
>   for your voice is sweet,

and your face is comely.
...

My beloved is mine and I am his,
...

I will seek him whom my soul loves.
...

   I found him whom my soul loves.
I held him, and would not let him go.
...

I adjure you,...
   if you find my beloved,
that you tell him
   I am sick with love.
...

for love is strong as death,
...

Many waters cannot quench love,
   neither can floods drown it.
If a man offered for love
   all the wealth of his house,
     it would be utterly scorned. (Song of Songs 2:13–14, 16;
3:2b, 4; 5:8; 8:6–7)

But why such pining and yearning and longing? Where does it all come from?

St. Basil the Great (+379) says this: "In receiving God's commandment of love, we immediately, from the first moment of our existence, possess the ability to love. The command does not come from outside of us...; it is a part of our nature to seek what is beautiful."[10] And the consummate beauty that our hungry heart seeks, as the author of the Song of Songs relates so well, is God's love.

St. Augustine (+430) makes a similar point:

We cannot love unless someone has loved us first.... The source of man's love for God can only be found in the fact that God loved him first.... This love is not something we generate ourselves; it comes to us *through the Holy Spirit who has been given to us....*

[God] cries out: Love me...for you would be unable to love me if you did not possess me already.[11]

This is why Pope Benedict XVI insists that "the human being lives on truth and on being loved: on being loved by the truth. He needs God, the God who draws close to him, interprets for him the meaning of life, and thus points him toward the path of life."[12] That drive in us is inescapable.

Because nothing can deceive the heart. No matter how hard we try to divert it, douse it, deny it, or divide it, the heart keeps after us, beleaguering us, pestering us as would a little kid to surrender to the Only Thing that will suffice. The heart knows what it needs.

When I'm stuck in the hamster wheel of futilely pursuing possessions, pleasure, power, and prestige, the resulting *disappointment* points me toward my desire—my destiny. I foolishly presume those four *p* things are not answers...but so often I enlist them as drugs to distract me from The Question: *When shall I behold the face of God?*

I am convinced that seeing his face, being held in his gaze, is the *only* thing that matters—is *everything*. To be human is to be wanted by Someone greater than I am.

Everything in my experience tells me that I have been *loved* into existence. Who is the One who loved me before I was born? Who is this One whose love is the very cause of my being? I cannot rest until I meet him, and know him, and embrace him as a friend. I have to see his face and hear his voice. My heart is restless, St. Augustine echoes through the ages, until it rests in him.[13]

REDEEMING LOVE

Servant of God Msgr. Luigi Giussani (+2005), the founder of the ecclesial movement Communion and Liberation, once wrote, "Man's need for the Mystery to reply to the ultimate human question is experienced as a manifestation of the Mystery itself."[14] Which means that, even if I say I don't believe in God, I cannot deny *him* without denying something vital in *myself*. I may try to "kill" God, but I can never kill the question *that I am*—a question to which only the Mystery—God!—is the Answer.

What do we call receiving the answer to that burning, relentless question? Redemption!

In his beautiful encyclical on hope, Pope Benedict XVI says:

> When someone has the experience of a great love in his life, this is a moment of "redemption" which gives a new meaning to his life.... The human being needs unconditional love.... If this absolute love exists, with its absolute certainty, then— only then—is man "redeemed," whatever should happen to him in his particular circumstances. This is what it means to say: Jesus Christ has "redeemed" us. Through him we have become certain of God....
>
> Man's great, true hope which holds firm in spite of all disappointments can only be God—God who has loved us and who continues to love us "to the end" (John 13:1).... If we are in relation with him who does not die, who is Life itself and Love itself, then we are in life. Then we "live."[15]

Fr. Julián Carrón, the president of Communion and Liberation, expresses the same thing in different words: "Inside all the ugliness and toil that you feel, if someone breaks in who loves you and you are surprised to find yourself loved and wanted...you want to participate in the adventure with this person who loves you."[16]

Would that Madalyn Murray O'Hair had said yes to this Someone who was trying to break in with his love through that wound in her heart. Thank God for the breakthrough gaze of Jesus that rescued Peter from the terrible ugliness of his betrayal so that he could later profess to the risen Lord, "You know that I love you" (John 21:17).

And God will not cease hounding *you* to surrender and share in the adventure of his love. As the *Catechism of the Catholic Church* teaches,

> At every time and in every place, God draws close to man. He calls man to seek him, to know him, to love him with all his strength.
>
> God never ceases to draw man to himself. Only in God will he find the truth and happiness he never stops searching for. (*CCC*, 1, 27)

The wound in us that moves us to cry out for love is a blessing. In his monumental work *Treatise on the Love of God*, doctor of the Church St. Francis de Sales (+1622) comments, "The cherubim were placed at the gate of the earthly paradise with their flaming sword to teach us that no one shall enter into the heavenly paradise who is not pierced through with the sword of love."[17] That piercing is our permit to heaven.

"Only the great certitude of hope that my own life and history in general despite all failures are held firm by the indestructible power of Love, and that this gives them their meaning and importance, only this kind of hope can then give the courage to act and to persevere."[18] We verify these arresting words of Pope Benedict XVI simply by paying attention to what our heart tells us. Love *is* greater than my failures or my problems. I *will* persevere and not give way to despair, because I have been pierced with a "great hope: 'I am definitively loved and whatever happens to me—I am awaited by this Love. And so my life is good.'"[19]

Drawn by the irresistible allure of an indestructible Love, we do what the anonymous author of the English mystical treatise *The Cloud of Unknowing* has been counseling since the fourteenth century: Lift up your heart to God with a gentle stirring of love and turn your mind over totally to the God who created you, who redeemed you, and who has graciously called you to this work of contemplating him (chapter seven).

To neglect this won't leave us unscathed. We then fall prey to what Duchess Dorothea of Prussia (+1580) dolefully prayed: "I actually wished that You might not exist rather than that I should continue to be tormented by You."[20]

For as agonizing as the torment of God's presence may in fact be, his absence is even worse. It's what we call *loneliness*.

THE GREATEST HUMAN MISERY

Cardinal Joseph Ratzinger once asked,

> In what does man's wretchedness actually consist?.... We can say...that the root of man's wretchedness is loneliness, is the absence of love—is the fact that my existence is not embraced by a love that makes it necessary, that is strong enough to justify it despite all the pain and limitations it imposes.[21]

We know this is so when we reflect on what sin does to us. "The effect [of sin] on the soul," wrote Dominican spiritual master Bede Jarrett, "is to be measured neither by the guilt nor by the temporal punishment inexorably affixed, but by that deep sense of loneliness it brings with it.... [Sin] makes a man realize as nothing else does the terrible loneliness of life."

Fr. Jarrett goes on to give the example of children who, after having done something wrong, find it hard to go back where they left off with their friends and revive the former joy of playing together. They have somehow severed themselves from such companionship. Sin alienates us, isolates us.

> Man...was made for love....
>
> By sin is all this love dried up. The parched and thirsty soul feels, therefore, the need of the dew of God, and rushes madly as the beasts wander in the jungle looking for the water they cannot find. The soul by sin is thus made solitary.... When I am feeling particularly the loneliness of life, perhaps the cause is that I lean too little upon God; perhaps it is that my sins will not let me feel that inward presence that is the sole real source of peace here below. I was created by Love for love, and when by sin I act contrary to Love, my heart must necessarily feel his absence.[22]

No wonder, then, that the worst possible punishment imaginable is solitary confinement.

Do you remember that bizarre television show from the 1990s called *Twin Peaks*? One episode was weirder than the next. But a particular scene stands out for me.

Major Garland Briggs of the U.S. Air Force, whose mission is highly classified, goes walking in the woods near Twin Peaks. The evil Windham Earle tracks him and paralyzes him with a tranquilizer dart. He ties Briggs to a huge target, arms outstretched cruciform. Earle shoots at him with a crossbow. Then he draws close and asks the major this question: "Garland, what do you fear most in the world?" Without hesitation Major Briggs responds, "The possibility that love is not enough."[23]

Truly that is the most terrifying thing in the world. Think of the kiss that Judas Iscariot gives to Jesus in the Garden of Gethsemane (see Matthew 26:49). Why are we shocked and scandalized, so devastated by it? Yes, it is a kiss by which Judas betrays his Lord. But that is not all. The kiss seems to be a betrayal of love itself. This tender gesture of love comes across as a hideous paradox—a despairing, mocking act that says: *Love is not enough, and so I hand you over to the darkness of evil.* But we know from the pitiful way that Judas's life ends that even he could not deal with the ensuing loneliness.

Studies show that loneliness takes a physical toll on us. In the book *Loneliness: Human Nature and the Need for Social Connection*, John T. Cacioppo (a professor of social neuroscience at the University of Chicago) and William Patrick (a science editor) point out that social isolation has an impact on health comparable to the effect of high blood pressure, lack of exercise, obesity, and smoking. Loneliness shows up in measurements of stress hormones, immune function, and cardiovascular function. Loneliness makes us sick! Even more, it can provoke physiological events that actually accelerate the aging process.[24]

Solitude or solitariness is not necessarily the culprit here but rather the chronic *feelings* of isolation. And loneliness can in fact be measured. To do so, researchers use a psychological assessment tool called the UCLA Loneliness Scale, consisting of twenty questions. The telling questions highlight what the heart requires to be whole, which goes well beyond simply "not being alone":

> How often do you feel that you lack companionship?
> How often do you feel that there is no one you can turn to?
> How often do you feel that you are no longer close to anyone?
> How often do you feel that your interests and ideas are not shared by those around you?
> How often do you feel that your relationships with others are not meaningful?
> How often do you feel that no one knows you well?

How often do you feel that people are around you but not with you?[25]

Cacioppo and Patrick note that when people are asked to list the pleasures that contribute most to happiness, the overwhelming majority name love, intimacy, and social affiliation, placing them ahead of wealth, fame, and even physical health.[26]

The authors also observe that, in the English language, we have words for pain and for thirst but not words that mean the opposites of those things. Instead we simply indicate their absence, because their absence is considered part of our normal state. The same is true of "loneliness"—there is no single term to express its opposite. And that's an optimistic reality. "Health and well-being for a member of our species requires, among other things, being satisfied and secure in bonds with other people, a condition of 'not being lonely' that, for want of a better word, we call social connection."[27]

Myself, I would prefer the word *communion*, à la Servant of God Dorothy Day (+1980) in her book *The Long Loneliness*: "We have all known the long loneliness and we have learned that the only solution is love and that love comes with community."[28]

Loneliness not only leads to an early grave; it also defines one mode of life beyond the grave: hell. Joseph Ratzinger, in his masterpiece *Introduction to Christianity*, speaks of loneliness as being "in fundamental contradiction with the nature of the human being, who cannot exist alone; he needs company."[29]

When we fall into extreme loneliness, we are not afraid of something definite that can be explained away. The anguish of it all consists in experiencing the *fear* of loneliness—the uneasiness and vulnerability of our human nature bereft of the *presence* of someone who loves us. Loneliness cannot be overcome with our minds. Which brings us to Ratzinger's definition of hell:

If there were such a thing as a loneliness that could no longer be penetrated and transformed by the word of another; if a state of abandonment were to arise that was so deep that no "You" could reach into it any more, then we should have real, total loneliness and dreadfulness, what theology calls "hell." We can now define exactly what this word means: it denotes a loneliness that the word love can no longer penetrate and that therefore indicates the exposed nature of existence in itself.[30]

But there *is* a Word that can penetrate and transform loneliness! From the first moment that this "Word became flesh and dwelt among us" (John 1:14) in the womb of the Blessed Virgin Mary—even before he developed the physical facility of speech—this Word speaks to us in the desolation of our abandonment and alienation. He says:

Come to me, all who labor and are heavy laden, and I will give you rest. (Matthew 11:28)

Blessed are the poor in spirit...
Blessed are those who mourn...
Blessed are the meek...
Blessed are those who hunger and thirst for righteousness...
Blessed are those who are persecuted...
Blessed are you when men revile you and persecute you and utter all kinds of evil against you falsely on my account. (Matthew 5:3, 4, 5, 6, 10, 11)

Take heart, it is I; have no fear. (Matthew 14:27)

I have called you friends.... You did not choose me, but I chose you. (John 15:15, 16)

This is my body which is given for you. (Luke 22:19)

I am with you always, to the close of the age. (Matthew 28:20)

In God's awesome, divine providence, even loneliness serves a salutary purpose. "I like to think of loneliness," writes Servant of God Catherine de Hueck Doherty (+1985), "as if it is a person with a particular job to do.... Loneliness brings us closer to Christ."[31]

WHAT TO DO ABOUT OUR NEED

This is certainly true of the leper in the Gospel. Despite the horror, the nightmare, that was his life, this tortured, mutilated man did not give up. The leper continued to live with a persistent, driving expectation. The loneliness of his misery led the leper to believe that there was something behind it all—a greater plan. He was convinced that he was not the sum total of his disease.

This conviction made him constantly scan the horizon for Someone—Someone whose love was strong enough to justify his wretched existence, even despite all its revulsion, and pain, and deformity. Someone whose love would embrace the leper's existence—as putrid as it was!—and tell him, *It is necessary that you exist!* The leper understood with all his being that he was not made for loneliness.

Which is why, when Jesus finally appeared on the road, the leper did not put his confidence in the *ability* of Jesus Christ but rather in his *desire*: "Lord, if you will, you can make me clean" (Matthew 8:2) is not a question; it is a statement, a judgment, a claim—a certainty that radiates from the heart of a man who at last is in the presence of the One for whom his heart is made.

The genius, the glory of the leper is that he trusts in the tenderness and generosity of Jesus's heart even when everything in the world tells him he has absolutely no right to do so. This is the fruit of *faith*, which is "the love of the heart of God who confides himself to our heart." (Fr. Maurice Zundel, +1975).[32] It blesses the leper with *the capacity to love*, which Pope Benedict XVI describes as "the capacity to wait in patience for what is not under one's own control and to let oneself receive this as a gift."[33]

In our starving for love, we need to do what the leper does: to cry out in faith to the One who put that hunger in us. As Hans Urs von Balthasar expresses it:

> Faith means the fundamental response to the love that has offered itself up for me.... Faith is ordered to...God's love, which surpasses us and anticipates us.... The "work" of faith [is] to recognize..., to believe that there is such a thing as long, absolute love, and that there is nothing higher or greater than it.[34]

Nothing higher or greater—not even our leprosy.

This beautiful prayer by St. Gregory of Narek helps us to carry this out:

> It is not for his gifts
> that I continue in my prayers,
> but because he is true Life.
>
> It is not so much by hope
> as by bonds of love that I am drawn.
> It is not for gifts,
> but for the Giver that I ever yearn.
>
> It is not glory I aspire to,
> but it is the Glorified One whom I wish to embrace.
> It is not by the desire for life,
> but by the remembrance of him who gives life
> that I am ever consumed!
> It is not for joyous passions that I yearn,

but it is because of a desire for him who is preparing them
that my heart bursts out in tears.
It is not rest that I seek,
but it is the face of him who offers rest
that I seek in prayer.

It is not for the nuptial banquet,
but it is for the Bridegroom that I long.
Despite the weight of my transgressions
I believe with an indubitable hope,
trusting in the hand of the Almighty One
that not only shall I obtain pardon,
but that I shall see him in person,
thanks to his mercy and pity,
and that I shall inherit heaven
although I completely deserve to be banished.

...Receive with sweetness,
O powerful Lord God,
the prayer of him who was bitterness for you.
...Grant that through remembrance of your hope
I may remain unscathed, protected by
You. Amen.[35]

CHAPTER TWO

God Is Love

God has not created us for human loving
but for that eternal awesome love
with which he loves everything
that he has ever created.

If you forget Love you make yourself absurd;
if you betray Love you become monstrous.
…
Love is our life becoming eternal life.[36]

—Servant of God Madeleine Delbrêl

I was once at a talk where I heard the Irish journalist John Waters say, "Fatherhood is only visible in its absence."[37] We want to understand what the love of God is; the nature of that love is a massive mystery. Maybe the insight of Mr. Waters applies to God's love as well: Maybe we understand it best when we miss it. Then it becomes visible.

For example, one of my favorite plays (and films) is Ronald Harwood's *The Dresser*. It's about a ragtag British Shakespearean troupe touring England during the Blitz of the Second World War. The director of the repertory company—simply called "Sir"—is a true *tour de force* as an actor. But his private life is in shambles, and his health is rapidly deteriorating. In fact, Sir's career in the theatre would be over if not for the dutiful ministrations of his personal dresser, Norman, who devises miraculous ways to keep propping him back up.

But middle-aged Norman has problems of his own: He is high-strung, adolescent, prone to outbursts, compulsive, alcoholic, psychologically touched, with a murky past. One wonders how Norman would ever get by in the world without this job, where people for some reason put up with him.

And then the worst thing possible happens: The seemingly immortal Sir suddenly, unexpectedly dies. Norman's initial stun and shock quickly morph into outrage over Sir's perpetual ingratitude, over sixteen insufferable years of self-absorption and inconsiderateness, over the fact that now *he* will be put out on the street. But despite all his justifiable rage, something even greater rises up through Norman's fury, taking hold of him. Norman thinks he is speaking to the company's stage manager (but she leaves the room) when he says:

> We all have our little sorrows, ducky, you're not the only one. The littler you are, the larger the sorrow. You think *you* loved him? What about me? *(Long silence)* This is not a place for death. I had a friend—[38]

A clue given early in the play hints that, years ago, Norman maybe was in a mental institution when, out of the blue, "a friend" sent a telegram with an offer of work—salvation. As Norman's hostility turns to tears, we wonder if Sir was the friend who acted in such a godlike way. It isn't until now, when his friend is dead, that Norman sees the love that he cannot live without. God's love is visible in its absence.

Or take another example: Tennessee Williams's play *A Streetcar Named Desire*. It is 1947. Blanche DuBois comes to New Orleans to stay at the French Quarter apartment of her younger, pregnant sister, Stella, who is married to the brutish Stanley.

Blanche is another complicated character. An aging Southern belle with a lurid past, snobbish and pretentious and seductive, teetering on insanity, Blanche is someone who evokes both pity and terror. Her ultimate nervous breakdown comes by way of a nightmarish confrontation with Stanley.

But before things turn bad, Blanche goes out on a date with one of Stanley's buddies, Mitch. Somehow Blanche plucks up the courage to divulge the most damning secret from her past, expecting immediate condemnation from Mitch. Instead he tells her, "You need somebody. And I need somebody, too." And Blanche responds, "Sometimes— there's God—so quickly!" The experience of helplessness, of need, of the abyss, makes God's love visible.

So too at the end of the play, when Blanche's mental collapse becomes complete. Stanley commits her to a mental institution. As a kindly doctor comes to take her away, Blanche looks up and says, "Whoever you are, I have always depended on the kindness of strangers." [39]

Haven't we all? And it isn't until that kindness is absent that we see just how much we need it—to an infinite degree.

Some may doubt the existence of God, but when things go from bad to worse, the only thing that keeps us going is the certainty that somehow, somewhere there is that stranger bearing us a kindness we can depend on. God is the stranger. God is the kindness we crave. "God is love" (1 John 4:8).

THE NATURE OF LOVE

What moves both our will and our appetites is love. For as St. Thomas Aquinas teaches, "Nobody desires anything nor rejoices in anything, except as a good that is loved.... In whomsoever there is will and appetite, there must also be love." [40]

That's why, in choosing our vacation destination, it is never a toss-up between Hawaii and a toxic waste dump. When you open a menu, you don't look for what you hate but for what you love. Even when we choose to sin, it is because we perceive in that sin some apparent good that we love. Everything that acts, whatever it may be, says St. Thomas, performs every action from some kind of love.[41]

Think about it: Why do you get excited over a delicious pan of lasagna straight from the oven...or the chance to spend a summer day at the beach...or tickets to a baseball game? Because you love all those things. We rejoice in wonderful things because we love them. To say that something is good, is desirable is the same as calling it lovable. We're always going after good things because we are made for love.

St. Thomas explains further:

> An act of love always tends towards two things; to the good that one wills, and to the person for whom one wills it: since to love a person is to wish that person good.... So love is called the unitive force, even in God.... For the good that he wills for himself, is no other than himself.... By the fact that anyone loves another, he wills good to that other. Thus he puts the other, as it were, in the place of himself; and regards the good done to him as done to himself.... Love is a binding force, since it [joins] another to ourselves, and refers his good to our own.... The divine love is a binding force. [42]

So when we say that God is love, we are making the claim that God by definition is One who wills good to us. And the good that God wills to us is not simply something he *has* but rather who he *is*— himself. God is love: He is the unifying, binding force whose will is to join us to himself in the greatest possible intimacy.

The delight, the joy, the fulfillment, the satisfaction, the meaning, the tenderness, the forgiveness, the newness, the happiness that our will and our appetites drive us to seek and find is nothing other than God himself.

As the poet Cesare Pavese put it, "What a man seeks in his pleasures is infinite and no one would ever give up hope of attaining that infinity."[43] In our pleasures we are looking for the good; the good is what we love. Our search for pleasure will not let us settle for anything less than infinite good. To speak of the infinite is to speak of God; and God reveals himself to be love. Since we are made for love, in pursuing pleasures we are actually going after God, the highest, supreme good. Our hope of attaining the infinite is identical with *who we are*.

So goes the line commonly attributed to G.K. Chesterton: Every man who knocks on the door of a brothel is looking for God.

How have we come to this certainty about God and the love that he is? Simply by paying attention to our *experience*. In his encyclical on the love of God, Pope Benedict XVI writes, "Love is not merely a sentiment.... God does not demand of us a feeling which we ourselves are incapable of producing. He loves us, he makes us see and experience his love, and since he has 'loved us first,' love can also blossom as a response within us."[44]

And if it is true what St. Thomas Aquinas says—that every person's life consists in the affection that principally sustains him and in which he finds his greatest satisfaction[45]—then the key to happiness consists in discovering and clinging to that affection that unfailingly sustains us and generates the greatest possible satisfaction. And that is our affection for God, for God is the very author of our affections. God is love.

But so often we succumb to faulty notions of God's love, tarnishing it, turning it into something it's not, or believing it is too good to be true. Or we plain forget about his love. Which is why it helps to have a few reminders regarding what makes the love of God so distinctive—so amazing.

GOD LOVES US BECAUSE HE IS GOOD

Think about your friends. Why did you choose them; why do you prefer them over other peers in your crowd? Clearly because you saw in them something attractive, some virtue that edified you, some attribute that appealed to you, a character trait that made you want to stay close.

God loves us for *exactly the opposite* reason. His love does not start with us; it starts with *him*. The motive for his loving us has nothing to do with anything attractive about us. Julian of Norwich wrote: "Before God made us he loved us."[46] As God says to St. Catherine of Siena, "Without having been loved by you, I loved you unspeakably much."[47] We can add: Without seeing anything lovable in us, God has loved us unspeakably much.

God's love *causes* goodness in us.

Go back to the rich young man. When he presents himself to Jesus, asking to inherit eternal life, he attempts to impress and sway Jesus with all his virtues and accomplishments and his perfect Ten Commandments report card. But here is the Lord's response: "One thing you still lack. Sell all that you have...and come, follow me" (Luke 18:22).

Mark prefaces Jesus's response to the rich man with "And Jesus looking upon him loved him" (Mark 10:21). Jesus does not love the man because of what he has or because of what he has done. And until the rich young man understands that, his very notion of God and eternal life will be illusory and depressing—a myth. Jesus loves the rich young man because Jesus is good, not because the man is good. The one thing the man lacks is knowledge of this crucial truth.

This is why the Lord demands that the man become poor. Because without divesting himself of everything—especially his grandiose self-satisfaction and sense of entitlement—the rich young man will wallow in the delusion that Jesus loves him and rewards him because of something good Christ sees in him. Love as a business deal. And the man will be inclined to keep trying (vainly) to earn, merit, and contract with God's love. He constantly will have to devise new ways of enticing and bedazzling God so that God might want him.

Selling everything that he has and giving it to the poor would bring on an induced poverty. Only in the lived experience of that poverty can the man see his accomplishments in their true light. For poverty makes us depend. As St. Thérèse of Lisieux (+1897), doctor of the Church, observes, "Poverty consists in being deprived not only of agreeable things but of indispensable things too."[48] The "poor young man" would see that he had actually accomplished nothing without depending on the One who brought him into existence, who provided him the oxygen he needs to breathe, who gave him food without which he would starve to death, and more.

In his self-congratulation the rich man has lost sight of the total destitution that he *is* left to himself. For there would be no "himself." Only indigence can show him the Someone who keeps him in existence moment by moment via a mercy that has nothing to do with what the man "deserves." Indeed, in comparison to such divine mercy, generosity, and grace, the man's mortal attainments appear for what they really are: nothing. *He* is nothing.

It seems almost scandalous that Jesus wants us *most* when we are utterly destitute: *Then* come and follow me. But isn't this the whole point of the Beatitudes? The ones whom Jesus calls "blessed" are the poor, the mourning, the hungry, the persecuted—that is, those who are nothing.

All this may make us doubtful about the existence of good taste in God. But so be it. Because any humble person will recognize that there is *nothing* we can do to make ourselves "good enough" for God. Yet this does not cause in us sorrow but rather joy, because *God loves to be acknowledged by nothingness.*

St. Thérèse of Lisieux says eloquently,

> Perfection seems simple to me, I see it is sufficient to recognize one's nothingness and to abandon oneself as a child into God's arms.... When he sees we are very much convinced of our nothingness, God extends his hand to us. If we still wish to attempt to do something *great* even under the pretext of zeal, Good Jesus leaves us all alone.... Yes, it suffices to humble oneself, to bear with one's imperfections. That is real sanctity![49]

We cannot allure God, we cannot court God, we cannot woo God. God woos us. Every day we should remind Jesus what he said to us the night he gave us his Body to eat: "You did not choose me, but I chose you" (John 15:16). We can come up with a thousand reasons for thinking his is a bad choice. Let them go. Happiness consists in living the conviction that Jesus chooses *you*. Happiness means trusting the reasons for what seems to be Christ's "crazy" choice.

One of my responsibilities as a priest is to run a theatre company in New York City for my Dominican province. Over the years I had been told about a devout Catholic man who was endeavoring to do something similar—my now friend Peter Dobbins, the director of the Storm Theatre. People kept saying that we definitely needed to meet each other, that we had so much in common.

Time went by, and circumstances at last put us together. However, as we finally sat face-to-face, I think we were a little wary of each other: Could we both *really* be on the same page when it came to faith, and theatre, and professionalism? We talked about plays and playwrights, productions and theories of the theatre.

At a certain point, who can remember why, the conversation turned to religion. And Peter started telling me about a play he admired because of the way it depicts God—God who loves us with this "crazy love." That did it: I was sold. Anyone who believes in God's crazy love is someone I need to be my friend. Forever.

We are all a little bit like Zacchaeus (see Luke 19:1–10). Zacchaeus had multiple reasons to believe he was not "eligible" for Jesus's love. As a tax collector he had sold out his integrity, compromising both his Jewish religion and fidelity to his nation. In the eyes of his fellow residents from Jericho, Zacchaeus was a public sinner—a pariah. Added to that, Zacchaeus was "small of stature"—maybe he had a problem with self-esteem?

Despite it all, Zacchaeus still "sought to see who Jesus was" (Luke 19:3). So to get a better vantage point, and perhaps to avoid being heckled and humiliated, Zacchaeus ran ahead of the crowd surrounding Jesus and climbed up into a sycamore tree. That is when the unexpected happened. "When Jesus came to the place, he looked up and said to him, 'Zacchaeus, make haste and come down; for I must stay at your house today'" (Luke 19:5).

God does not love us because we are good but because he is. Jesus is the one who stops in his tracks, who looks at us in the very place where we are trying to hide from him, who calls to us with an invitation of love, and who stays with us, even though there are a thousand "better" places where the Lord could choose to stay.

Let's make haste, come down from our excuses, and receive Jesus joyfully, every day.

God Loves Us Just the Way We Are

When does Jesus appear to St. Paul on the road to Damascus and reveal his divine plan for him as "a chosen instrument of mine…to carry my name before the Gentiles and kings and the sons of Israel" (Acts 9:15)? Precisely when Saul/Paul is "still breathing threats and murder against the disciples of the Lord" (Acts 9:1). Jesus comes and claims Paul for himself at the point when Paul is at his absolute worst, when he is a rabid enemy of Jesus Christ and of his Church.

God who is love wants us just the way we are right now.

One tricky pastoral task each Holy Week involves rounding up twelve volunteers willing to get their feet washed at the Mass of the Lord's Supper on Holy Thursday night. My experience is that people generally shy away from this. Something about it makes many squeamish, uncomfortable. No problem, I suppose, if the priest wanted to wash some other more noble or dignified body part. But there's something awkward and mortifying about letting another person wash our feet.

Why? Because deep down we remain resistant to letting ourselves be loved just the way we are, with all our grime and odor, warts and hammertoes. Even when it is God himself in the person of Christ, kneeling before us in an apron with a basin, we draw back, as if to say, *Love me, but not in this way.*

And as we recoil from the hands of God stretched out toward our feet, we may even feel some righteous indignation, as did St. Peter: "You shall never wash my feet" (John 13:8). That reaction implies that Christ's gesture is not merely unseemly but actually *wrong!* Has Jesus forgotten who he is? What could God be thinking? Maybe he should take some lessons from us about the right way to love us.

But no: God's method of loving us is infinitely better than the one in our mind. Even more, we *need* his love precisely to overcome the weakness in our reasoning caused by original sin. St. Thérèse of Lisieux once lamented: "Jesus finds few hearts who surrender to him without reservation, who understand the real tenderness of his infinite love."[50]

Jesus knows how we can be: like those people who madly rush around cleaning the house on the morning that the maid is coming to clean the house. We are ashamed to let others see our mess. We can't bear to let others think badly about us.

That's the thing in us that needs to be fixed. Only God's love—in the manner God chooses to love us—can fix it. The last thing God wants is for us to try to fix ourselves up before allowing him into our lives.

One of the great mysteries of the faith—and now of the rosary—is the baptism of the Lord (see Mark 1:9–11). Did you ever wonder why someone who never sinned, who doesn't even possess the proclivity to sin (concupiscence), and who is personally a member of the Blessed Trinity would present himself for baptism? Doesn't it seem like a pretty superfluous thing to do? A waste of time and energy? Yet Jesus does so as the inaugural act of his public ministry.

So what is the purpose of his baptism? Jesus wants our first impression of him to be that of someone just like us. We're at the Jordan River, waiting our turn with the other sinners. As we slowly inch our way to John the Baptist, next to us stands a man named Jesus. Although he is God, he comes disguised as a sinner like ourselves: "For our sake [God] made him to be sin" (2 Corinthians 5:21). Through this experience Jesus wants to show us—prove to us—how much he wants to get close to us just the way we are and how much we need his *presence* to overcome our resistance and our reluctance toward his love.

Jesus will always devise surprising ways to subvert our aversion to his loving us. The flaws and defects that we feel to be such impossible impediments are the very things he asks us to hand over. *The best way to go to him is with our corruption!*

This truth of God's love demands from us a profound act of faith. Because it reveals just how all-encompassing God's divine providence truly is. We are the way we are right now because God's providence permits us to be that way right now. Somehow God ordains to use our current condition—even an incredibly sinful one—to be the breakthrough occasion for his love. All we have to give him is our self of the present moment. He begs us to trust that who we are right now is part of a plan that leads to the full embrace of his love.

Of course, God in his goodness does not leave us the way we are, especially if it entails being ensnared in sin. But the process of our purification and perfection begins in entrusting ourselves to God right now, just the way we are, with confidence.

Think again about the Samaritan woman at the well. In the course of her encounter with Jesus, the Lord divulges to her the most despicable sins of her life: "You have had five husbands, and he whom you now have is not your husband" (John 4:18). Why would Jesus say something so potentially off-putting? Doesn't he risk making the woman feel condemned by her sin?

But what if she were to leave Jesus's presence without hearing these words? Her initial elation would eventually fade and sour. The weight of her shame would reassert itself, and the woman would think: *If Jesus knew the way I* really *am, he would never love me.*

The only way out of sin's blackmail is to let God love us just the way we are. Because his love is infinitely greater than our evil.

Only God's Love Makes Us Worthy of God's Love

> Ho, every one who thirsts,
>   come to the waters;
> and he who has no money,
>   come, buy and eat!
> Come, buy wine and milk
>   without money and without price. (Isaiah 55:1)

Only the gift of God's love, given freely to us when we deserve it the least, can make us worthy of God's love. God is not dissuaded by what we do not have. What makes us worthy of attending the feast is his desire for us to be there. His invitation to our humility is simple:

Accept the feast of my love so that you will be worthy to attend the feast of my love.

A true story by way of example. In a certain city where I lived for a time there was a very elite country club. Not only was membership restricted to the rich, but the bylaws stipulated a certain peculiar rule. In order to belong, the establishment dictated that an applicant's income be *inherited*, not *made*.

One man eagerly intent on joining was an immigrant who was a self-made millionaire as well as a person of standing in the local community. His application was denied. But years later when his adult son applied to the same country club for membership, that man was accepted, because *his wealth was inherited*. Wacky.

Here's the thing: God's love is the club we want to belong to. What makes us worthy of God's love? Nothing of our own making. We can't earn, or barter, or bargain our way into membership. What then can we do? Are we doomed?

No—because our Father is holding out to us an incalculable inheritance. All he asks is that we be willing to receive it. Then we become worthy of membership. The club wants us.

As St. Paul writes, "If you are Christ's, then you are...heirs according to promise" (Galatians 3:29). And in another place, "When we cry, 'Abba! Father!' it is the Spirit himself bearing witness with our spirit that we are children of God" (Romans 8:15–16).

There's an analogy I always find helpful. You're a little kid, and Father's Day is coming up. You want to give your father a Father's Day card because you love him. But you have no money. So what do you do?

You go to your father and ask him to give you some money (he figures out why you want it!). Your father says yes, hands you the money, and you go out and buy your dad the most beautiful Father's Day card you can find. To this day it remains *the* best Father's Day present he's ever gotten from you. In fact, he still has it! It's in the top drawer of his dresser, all the way to the right, underneath the handkerchiefs, right?

Wait a minute: the *best gift ever?* Isn't it just a lousy card? No—much more. For the real gift is the *confidence* that penniless little you invest in your father by asking him to give you what you need so that you can give him the most perfect, worthy gift. It doesn't matter that the money you use to buy the card isn't yours. What does matter is that in order to love him well, you let your father love you first. He delights both in your desire to express your love for him and in your utter reliance on his bounty to make that happen.

St. Leo the Great teaches that the only way God can be worthily honored is by presenting him with what he has already given us.[51] The liturgy celebrates this grace. Common Preface IV declares, "Our thanksgiving is itself your gift."[52] In Eucharistic Prayer I we pray, "We, your servants and your holy people, offer to your glorious majesty, from the gifts that you have given us, this pure victim, this holy victim, this spotless victim."[53] And Eucharistic Prayer III: "May [Christ] make of us an eternal offering to you, so that we may obtain an inheritance with your elect."[54]

The patron saint of this aspect of God's love is the good thief (see Luke 23:39–43). He begs, "Jesus, remember me when you come in your kingly power." The good thief recognizes that there is no goodness in himself to attract Jesus. Yet he senses the furnace of love that is Christ's Sacred Heart, soon to be pierced. If Jesus will love the thief, the reason will be that Jesus is good, not that the thief is.

Moreover, Jesus will need to love the thief just the way he is. Even if the good thief were theoretically inclined to try to improve his condition before pleading for companionship with Christ, the nails fastening him to his cross (thankfully!) dash that chance. And the good thief clearly realizes that the only thing that will make him worthy of the love of heaven is the love of heaven living in this dying man beside him.

The good thief is perhaps the least "worthy" person on the planet to receive God's love. Yet all the same, it is to him that the Savior of the world declares, "Today you will be with me in Paradise."

In their mystical dialogue God says to St. Catherine of Siena: "I ask you to love me with the same love with which I love you."[55] The success of love depends on this nonnegotiable, as St. Thérèse of Lisieux intuits: "For me to love you, Jesus, as you love me, I would have to borrow your own love and then only would I be at rest."[56]

Wisdom dictates, then, the best way to proceed, as counseled by Servant of God Madeleine Delbrêl (+1964):

> We should…accept this love
> not as a large-hearted magnificent partner
> but as the idiot beneficiary of it that we are,
> devoid both of charm and basic loyalty.[57]

And we do so simply and confidently, taking up St. Columban's (+615) prayer:

> Loving Savior…inspire in us the depth of love that is fitting for you to receive as God. So may your love pervade our whole being, possess us completely, and fill all our senses, that we may know no other love but love for you who are everlasting.[58]

GOD LOVES US AS HE LOVES HIMSELF

How exactly does God love us?

The way we love our pet cocker spaniel? We find the dog cute and fluffy, such a great companion, and so fun to play with. But at a certain point, he becomes annoying, gets on our nerves, and it's time to put little Wrigley in the backyard for a while. Is that how God regards us?

Hurray, no. The shocking fact is that *God loves us the way that he loves himself.*

Jesus loves only what the Father has given him. God the Father has given *us* to him (see John 17:6–7). Since we belong to Jesus, Jesus cannot love himself without loving us. Therefore Jesus loves us as he loves himself. He loves us as an equal, wanting the chief thing that love brings forth, namely, union with others.

Jesus longs for union with us. Just remember the prayer that fills Christ's Sacred Heart the night before he dies: "[I pray] that they may all be one; even as you, Father, are in me, and I in you, that they also may be in us" (John 17:21).

Dom Aelred Graham, in his classic book *The Love of God*, helps us to understand this mystery:

> The supernatural love of God...is an elevation of the will to a manner of loving for which it has, from a natural viewpoint, no capacity at all. Just as the essence of the soul is adorned with sanctifying grace so that it participates in the divine nature, in parallel fashion, the will is divinized to enable it to love God and creatures, no longer merely naturally, but in the way in which God himself loves. Charity is something quite literally divine. It is a sharing by the creature in the mutual love of the Father and the Son. Through charity we show towards God the intimate affection wherewith he loves himself.[59]

One of the Lord's most magnificent—and misunderstood—parables is the parable of the talents (see Matthew 25:14–30). Preachers repeatedly exhort their hearers to "use their talents for the glory of God." A pious—and potentially Pelagian—sentiment. What does that platitude have to do with Jesus Christ? It gives the impression that we naturally possess what we need to please God. If that's the case, why was there ever an Incarnation?

Here's the problem with that interpretation: The talents in the parable are not *ours*; they belong to the *master*. Here's another problem: The talents aren't "talents" like skills, abilities, aptitudes, knacks; the talents are money, currency, coins. In fact, the talents are given to each servant *"according to his ability"* (Matthew 25:15). So clearly the talents are extrinsic somethings separate from intrinsic abilities. The degree of personal ability determines how many talents a servant receives.

Just what the master confides to these three lowest-class slaves is in fact a mind-numbing sum; just one talent had the value of more than fifteen years' worth of a laborer's wages. "Then he went away" for "a long time" (Matthew 25:15, 19).

Put yourself in the servants' sandals: You're a slave; you've just been given a king's ransom; the master who gave it to you is somewhere far away for who knows how long. Plus he didn't say a word to you about what to do with the cash—he uttered no instructions whatsoever. You have *absolutely no accountability!*

What do you do with the money? One word comes to *my* mind: Acapulco! Or if fleeing and starting life over elsewhere seems too extreme, at the very least I would use the money to buy myself out of servitude—manumission (which was done all the time, for example, Leviticus 25:49–50).

But the servants don't opt for the obvious. The first two invest the money. They stick around and keep working. All the while their capital accrues interest.

When "a long time" is over, and the master returns and wants to settle accounts with them, the first two servants obediently step forward. They present their original outlay along with the interest it has earned, which thrills the master. He says to each of them, "Well done, good and faithful servant; you have been faithful over a little, I will set you over much; enter into the joy of your master" (Matthew 25:21, 23).

Not "enter into the *pleasure* of your master," but rather "the *joy* of the your master." What does it mean to share another's joy? What is special about our relationship with someone whose joy has become our own?

At the very least, one *sine qua non* is *equality*. We must be on an equal footing with the offerer; otherwise there is no way for us to rejoice in that person's joy. In such a case, entering into another's joy would not be joyful; it would be work.

In the act of giving the servants the vast sum of money, it is as if the master entrusts them with what is most precious to him—his life savings. He loves them as he loves himself. For whom else would the master entrust with such a monumental amount of money except... *himself*!

The servants perceive this. Certainly one reason they do not run off with the windfall is because they divine the significance of the master's act: In treating donkey-dung shovelers like chief financial officers, the master elevates them to his own level. They feel loved by the master in the very way the master loves himself. They take up the master's challenge because "those who are loved enter fearlessly into the heart of their lover" (St. John Chrysostom).[60]

And what an exceptional master he is! His familiarity with the three servants is personal and attentive, sensitive and well-informed. The master knows that Servant Number One can handle five talents, while Servant Number Two is really only up to two. Come on, what CEO is like that? I can think of only one "master" who possesses such amazing insight and manifests such affectionate solicitude to the littlest who serve him: God the Father.

Which is why if you want to say that the parable is about using *God's* talents for the glory of God, well that's a different matter. And who can doubt that the master in the parable represents God?

But what do the *talents* symbolize? The key is in the Greek word used to describe the conferral of the funds: *paradidomi*, "hand over"—a theological term reserved in the New Testament for speaking about *Jesus Christ being handed over to his passion.* The talents are Jesus.

What is the master's purpose in this parable? Clearly it is not about increasing his income, because he doesn't even keep the revenue the servants return (see Matthew 25:28). The point of the parable is not about garnering assets but about gaining trust. The master sets up a kind of test to elicit confidence, devotion, and friendship from his servants. He wants to transform their very identity. Will the servants assess the master's heart and see what he is really after—their intimacy with him?

The master draws this response from them by loving them as he loves himself. "For God so loved the world that he gave his only-begotten Son, that whoever believes in him should not perish but have eternal life" (John 3:16). This drama of exorbitant loving gets played out symbolically in the parable of the talents. God's love asks only the privilege of giving itself to us, and that we be willing to receive it.

The parable asks, How do we respond to the Father's gift to us of his Son? What do we do with the Son of God who is handed over to us—even literally in the Eucharist at the Last Supper? For that gift is the sign of how much God loves us: as he loves himself. Our response to Jesus the Talents changes everything. Will we put our confidence in the confidence that the Father invests in us in handing over his Son to us? Or will we succumb to fear and cling to our servitude like the third servant?

Jesus in effect says to us: Look at the priceless treasure the master entrusts to his servants. See how in accepting it, in grasping its meaning, the treasure changes the way they look at the master and the way they look at themselves. See how the gift of the talents reveals to them abilities they never knew they had. The servants' entire desire is for the master. And the desire of the master is for them to enter into his joy. What God hands over on the cross is given to woo you away from your slavery and into the truth that he loves you as he loves himself: as his own son or daughter.

Lord Jesus, may I never cease to live in that silent, tender gaze of the Father, in which with lavish love he hands over to me his Everything, you. United with you in the Eucharist, may I hand myself over to the Father in a total gift of self. Account me a good and faithful servant—let me always live by faith in you.

God Is Our Father

The point of the parable of the talents is to convince us of one thing: The master is more than our master; he is our Father. Our vocation is to be children. We realize this through the gift of God's Son. The Father loves us as he loves him. The key to sanctity is spiritual childhood.

The whole of Christ's heart, mind, and soul is given over to leading us to the Father. The night before Jesus dies, he prays to the Father, "I made known to them your name, and I will make it known" (John 17:26). That same night the Lord promises, "I will not leave you desolate," and, "He who has seen me has seen the Father" (John 14:18, 9).

St. Hilary of Poitiers (+368) made the observation that the greatest work of the Son of God was to bring us to knowledge of the Father.[61] As the *Catechism of the Catholic Church* teaches, "Christ's whole earthly life—his words and deeds, his silences and sufferings, indeed his manner of being and speaking—is *Revelation* of the Father" (*CCC*, 516).

But original sin has made us forgetful of the fatherhood of God and thwarted our search for him. St. John Paul II wrote that one of the chief effects of original sin is that it "attempts to abolish father-hood,...placing in doubt the truth about God who is Love and leaving man only with a sense of the master-slave relationship."[62]

In contemporary society *father* has practically become a dirty word. All the same, life becomes unlivable if there is not a father present who loves us. Greg Bellow, the son of the Nobel-winning author Saul Bellow, recounts his reaction after his parents divorced and his father left the family: "I felt like a deep-sea diver cut off from my air supply."[63] Add to that what a prevalent motif the search for the father has been in literature and film over the centuries.

The father that we ultimately seek is the one who loves us infinitely, God the Father.

When the prodigal son reaches the end of his self-indulging spree, hits rock bottom, and comes to his senses, he doesn't decide to return to his brother, his girlfriend, or his therapist. No, he resolves, "I will arise and go to my father, and I will say to him, 'Father'" (Luke 15:18).

Why? Because what we require when caught in straits similar to the prodigal son's can be found only in the Father. What is so special about a father?

Pope Benedict XVI helps us understand:

> The word "Father" makes me sure of one thing: I do not come from myself; I am a child. I am tempted at first to protest against this reminder as the prodigal Son did. I want to be "of age", "emancipated", my own master. But then I ask myself: What is the alternative for me—or for any person—if I no longer have a Father, if I have left my

state as child definitively behind me? What have I gained thereby? Am I really free? No, I am free only when there is a principle of freedom, when there is someone who loves and whose love is strong. Ultimately, then, I have no alternative but to turn back again, to say "Father," and in that way to gain access to freedom by acknowledging the truth about myself.[64]

If we reflect on what makes human fatherhood so distinctive, we receive a tiny glimpse into the unfathomable love of God the Father. For as the author J.R.R. Tolkien once remarked in a letter to his son, "The link between father and son is not only of the perishable flesh: it must have something of *aeternitas* about it."[65]

A father is someone who loves you for one singular reason: because you are his. And for this same reason a father believes you are the best child in the world. That judgment is not based on what you can do but simply on the fact that you are his. At the same time a father knows full well the worst about you, and in that knowledge he loves you all the more because you *need* to be loved more, and what else can raise you up from what weighs you down but a father's love? This is why a father never becomes fatalistic about your failures. More than that, he believes you can do anything that he wishes, because a father wants *only what you can do*. Sometimes we don't know what we are capable of doing until a father loves us into our true selves.

Perhaps the one overarching quality of fatherhood that we yearn for in God is what Fr. Julián Carrón calls "passion for our nothingness":

> We are surprised by a person who has passion for our nothingness, because he looks at us without reducing us, with our whole need for happiness at heart. Someone who feels looked at like this immediately experiences the recoil that

makes him grasp how it corresponds: "This is what I was waiting for, someone who looked at me like this, who truly had my *I* at heart, who affirmed me like this, so that I could experience living like never before!"[66]

Joseph Campbell, author of *The Power of Myth*, reflecting on predominant themes in world mythologies, tells us that "the finding of the father has to do with finding your own character and destiny."[67] As Bishop Massimo Camisasca expresses it, "A father desires to help his child truly to 'meet' himself and what is around him. He wants to make him walk on the earth without forgetting the stars."[68]

In teaching us to pray Our Father, the Lord provides more than a method of prayer. The *Catechism of the Catholic Church* instructs, "The Lord's Prayer *reveals us to ourselves* at the same time that it reveals the Father to us" (CCC, 2783).

The inestimable privilege of being able to call God "Father" moves us to follow the profound counsel offered by Adrienne von Speyr:

> The person upon whom God lavishes himself ought to be seized by vertigo in such a way that he sees only the light of God and no longer his own limits, his own weakness. The person who sees only the light of God should renounce every equilibrium sought by himself, he should give up the idea of a dialogue between himself and God as between two partners and become a simple receiver with arms spread wide yet unable to grasp, because the light runs through everything and remains untouchable, representing much more than our own effort could receive.[69]

Put very simply, the reality of the fatherhood of God gives us the courage to live as spiritual children. The great Church doctor of spiritual childhood, St. Thérèse of Lisieux, urges us:

If God wants you to be as weak and powerless as a child, do you think your merit will be any less for that? Resign yourself, then, to stumbling at every step, to falling even, and to being weak in carrying your cross. Love your powerlessness, and your soul will benefit more from it than if, aided by grace, you were to behave with enthusiastic heroism—and fill your soul with self-satisfaction.[70]

And then, taking her own medicine, she professes in a prayer:

I expect each day to discover new imperfections in myself. I am simply resigned to see myself always imperfect—and in this I find my joy. My own folly is this: to trust that your love will accept me.... I am only a child, powerless and weak, and yet it is my weakness that gives me the boldness of offering myself as a victim of your love, O Jesus![71]

St. John Paul II sums up the tremendous mystery of the nature of God's love in one of his plays in which a character declares, "One must enter the radiation of fatherhood, since only there does everything become fully real."[72]

We beg for the grace to do just this as we pray with Blessed Elizabeth of the Trinity:

O my God, Trinity whom I adore; help me to forget myself entirely that I may be established in you as still and as peaceful as if my soul were already in eternity. May nothing trouble my peace or make me leave you, O my Unchanging One, but may each minute carry me further into the depths of your mystery. Give peace to my soul; make it your heaven, your beloved dwelling and your resting place. May I never leave you there alone but be wholly present, my faith wholly vigilant, wholly adoring, and wholly surrendered to your creative action.[73]

CHAPTER THREE

FRIENDSHIP WITH GOD

When my youthful heart was afire
with the flame we call love,
You came and claimed it for Yourself.
And You alone, O Jesus, could satisfy my soul,
for boundless was my need of loving You.[74]

—St. Thérèse of Lisieux

Nowhere in the Gospels does Jesus speak the words "I love you." It is not until the Last Supper, the night before he dies, that he says something along those lines: "As the Father has loved me, so have I loved you" (John 15:9). Yet throughout the Lord's public ministry, people are convinced that Jesus loves them. Why?

Msgr. Luigi Giussani defines friendship as *every relationship in which the other's need is shared in its ultimate meaning*.[75] Is it possible for us to live, even for five minutes, without someone like this in our life? As people in the Gospels encounter Jesus, they recognize a friend. For in meeting Christ they experience their need being shared in its ultimate meaning, maybe for the very first time.

More than anything else perhaps, this is what the Blessed Virgin Mary wants to impress upon the world at the wedding feast at Cana, when the wine runs out (see John 2:1–11). In directing the servants, "Do whatever he tells you" (John 2:5), Our Lady publicly identifies human need with her Son. Our deepest need, our truest thirst—the one that Jesus will identify himself with on the verge of death as he cries from the cross, "I thirst!" (John 19:28)—is now and forever shared in its ultimate meaning by this man. At a feast of love, the Mother of God reveals her Son to us as our friend.

Why else would the people bring to Jesus "all the sick, those afflicted with various diseases and pains, demoniacs, epileptics, and paralytics" (Matthew 4:24) but for the fact that in Jesus they have found someone who shares their need in its ultimate meaning? Something similar happens the second Jesus sets foot on the shore of Gennesaret: "The people recognized him, and ran about the whole neighborhood and began to bring sick people on their pallets to any place where they heard he was" (Mark 6:54–55).

When did Jesus call his first disciples, Simon and Andrew and James and John (see Matthew 4:18–22)? It was "when he heard that John [the Baptist] had been arrested" (Matthew 4:12). Did the experience of grief trigger in Jesus the craving for friends, friends who would become in turn lifelong companions?

Throughout the Gospels we encounter people whose lives are entirely caught up in waiting for Jesus. The four men whose friend is a paralytic go to the pains of removing the roof and lowering the pallet of their friend—*whom they have carried up to the roof*— through the opening, so convinced are they of the saving friendship of Jesus (see Matthew 9:1–8; Mark 2:1–12; Luke 5:17–26). Blind Bartimaeus, in the darkness of his suffering, nonetheless sees a hope worth crying out to: "Jesus, Son of David, have mercy on me!" (Mark 10:47). It is the cry of a friend summoning a friend. A similar confidence appears in the ten lepers: "Jesus, Master, have mercy on us" (Luke 17:11–13).

For others the experience of catastrophic suffering brings a breakthrough certainty about Jesus. They rush to him as to a friend— as to one longing to share their need in its ultimate meaning. The Canaanite woman begs, "Have mercy on me, O Lord, Son of David; my daughter is severely possessed by a demon" (Matthew 15:22). Jairus, the synagogue ruler, risking his reputation as well as public scandal, falls at the feet of Jesus imploring, "My little daughter is at the point of death. Come and lay your hands on her, so that she may be made well, and live" (Mark 5:23). A father emerges from a crowd to plead, "Teacher, I brought my son to you, for he has a mute spirit; and wherever it seizes him, it dashes him down; and he foams and grinds his teeth and becomes rigid" (Mark 9:17–18). And of course, Martha and Mary of Bethany, with their brother Lazarus on the verge of death, send this message to Jesus: "Lord, he whom you love is ill" (John 11:3). The evangelist John—who may well be the Beloved Disciple—comments, "Now Jesus loved Martha and her sister and Lazarus" (John 11:5).

How do we account for the profound conviction among these people that Jesus is someone they can rely on so radically...someone they can trust thoroughly, completely, as one only trusts a friend? Yes, they were looking for healing, liberation, relief. But even more, their circumstances moved them to look at their own selves—to take their *I* seriously.

We Are Made for Friendship
Pope Benedict XVI explains:

> Of ourselves, we cannot come to terms with ourselves. Our *I* becomes acceptable to us only if it has first become acceptable to another *I*. We can love ourselves only if we have first been loved by someone else.... It is only when life has been accepted and is perceived as accepted that it becomes also acceptable. Man is that strange creature that needs not just physical birth but also appreciation if he is to subsist.... If an individual is to accept himself, someone must say to him: "It is good that you exist"—must say it, not with words, but with that act of the entire being that we call love. For it is the way of love to will the other's existence and, at the same

51

time, to bring that existence forth again. The key to the *I* lies with the *you;* the way to the *you* leads through the *I.*[76]

We are made for friendship.

St. Aelred of Rievaulx (+1167) lauds the glory of friendship in his famous treatise on spiritual friendship:

> Friendship heightens the joys of prosperity and mitigates the sorrows of adversity by dividing and sharing them. Hence, the best medicine in life is a friend.... Not even water, nor the sun, nor fire do we use in more instances than a friend.... And so it is that the rich prize friendship as their glory, the exiles as their native land, the poor as their wealth, the sick as their medicine, the dead as their life, the healthy as their charm, the weak as their strength, and the strong as their prize.... Friendship is a stage bordering upon that perfection which consists in the love and knowledge of God, so that man from being a friend of his fellowman becomes a friend of God, according to the words of the Savior in the Gospel: "I will not now call you servants, but my friends."[77]

But how do we ever perceive the existence of a love like that? St. Thomas Aquinas tells us,

> At the present time we cannot know how great God's love for us is: this is because the good things that God will give us exceed our longings and desires, and so cannot be found in our heart....
>
> Thus the believing world, that is, the saints, will now know by experience how much God loves us.[78]

When people entrenched in their need—their woundedness, their longing—encountered Jesus Christ, what they experienced in his exceptional presence *corresponded* with the deepest yearnings of their hearts. That experience of correspondence moved them to confide themselves to the love radiating from Jesus Christ. It blessed them with the certainty that God himself was accepting and loving them through this man. That is why they approached this man and asked him, in friendship, to do for them what only God can do.

I was on a retreat many years ago with some young people in the Rocky Mountains. At the end of the retreat, we all had the chance to stand and share with the group some of the graces we had received. I remember one young woman coming forward and saying to us very simply, "I know that God loves me because he gives me companions." Then she sat down.

I was bowled over. It's true! The amazing friends I have: I didn't "find" them; I certainly don't deserve them; but I do have them. And there is only one feasible reason: because my friends are God's gift to me in proof of his love for me, his friendship.

And even though the good that God wills to give us ultimately exceeds our desires, our fundamental human need for friendship begins to show itself expressly *through* our desires. That is the vital experience by which we sense how God loves us. C.S. Lewis once observed, "Are not all lifelong friendships born at the moment when at last you meet another human being who has some inkling...of that something which you were born desiring.... Always it has summoned you out of yourself."[79]

This may explain why the first words of Jesus in the Gospel of John are "What do you seek?" (John 1:38).

In this vein St. Gregory the Great (+604) says that the nature of love is to rise each day higher above oneself toward God by holy desires and never to rest until one has reached the supreme good.[80]

The experience of desire keeps our heart, made as it is for infinite love, from ever compromising the ultimate satisfaction it seeks.

The author Saul Bellow captures the drama of this in his 1958 novel *Henderson the Rain King*:

> There was a disturbance in my heart, a voice that spoke there and said, *I want, I want, I want!* It happened every afternoon, and when I tried to suppress it it got even stronger. It only said one thing, *I want, I want!* And I would ask, "What do you want?" But this was all it would ever tell me. It never said a thing except *I want, I want, I want!* At times I would treat it like an ailing child whom you offer rhymes or candy. I would walk it, I would trot it. I would sing to it or read to it. No use.... No purchase, no matter how expensive, would lessen it. Then I would say, "Come on, tell me. What's the complaint?"... The demand came louder, *I want, I want, I want, I want, I want!* And I would cry, begging at last, "Oh, tell me then. Tell me what you want!"[81]

What we want is the miracle that Jesus makes happen in these words:

> Greater love has no man than this, that a man lay down his life for his friends. You are my friends if you do what I command you. No longer do I call you servants, for the servant does not know what his master is doing; but I have called you friends, for all that I have heard from my Father I have made known to you. (John 15:13–15)

This inestimable gift, friendship, is the love called *charity*. It is the love that never stops repeating with all its heart: "I want you to exist! It is good that you exist!"

Blessed Simon Fidati of Cascia (+1348) was an Augustinian friar whose renown as a brilliant preacher shines in this passage—an encomium to friendship:

A friend comes to the rescue in time of need, and...directs his friend just as if he were himself, and puts his own members at his disposal if he has lost his. A true friend is better than a treasure, for he is not vulnerable to thieves and robbers. A friend is a lighted coal, and if placed beside it, it can rekindle a dead one. A true friend gives more attention to friendship than to the person with whom he is disposed to be friendly. For indeed the person often disappoints, but the friendship is always the same....

Christian friendship...gives trust in life, a protection and a staff supporting even those who have shown weakness, a sure refuge, a haven from the sea, release from prison, freedom from slavery, an invaluable abode of divine protection, a tower of safety, a vineyard of joy, an ever fertile field, a pleasure garden of consolation, a repository of perfumes, a full storehouse, an apiary of honey...a mirror of brightness and an intellectual vision, a bride by one's side with whom the comforts of life are shared, a pious mother, an obliging attendant, a ready handmaid, a convenient bodyguard, a favorable bathing place, a spring of living water, an unsleeping guard against evil, prudence in the midst of good, a bond with life.[82]

THE SACRED HEART OF JESUS: THE EXPERIENCE OF GOD'S FRIENDSHIP

In many respects the Solemnity of the Sacred Heart is the "feast day" of Jesus. For as the *Directory on Popular Piety and the Liturgy* states, "the term 'Sacred Heart of Jesus' denotes the entire mystery of Christ."[83] Or to put it another way, what "defines" Jesus Christ is his Sacred Heart. We cannot know or understand the deepest truth of this man who is God apart from his Sacred Heart and all that that human heart signifies.

By identifying his very self with his Sacred Heart, Jesus reveals to the world his truest identity: He is forever the Son of the Father who lives to make of himself an unceasing and total gift of love. For the motivating intention of all the actions of the Sacred Heart of Jesus is to glorify God the Father by making him known, loved, and served—to bring forth our friendship with the Father. Through the mystery of the Sacred Heart, the Lord says in effect, *If you would desire to know me, then you must accept the gift of my love. For there can be no true knowledge of me apart from the love I long to impart to you.*

The pierced, open side of Christ on the cross, which makes visible the Sacred Heart of the Son of God, remains "the way in" to knowledge of Jesus Christ.

The feast of the Sacred Heart is the enshrinement, so to say, of Jesus's most heartfelt yearning in the Gospels: "Come to me, all who labor and are heavy laden, and I will give you rest. Take my yoke upon you, and learn from me; for I am gentle and lowly in heart, and you will find rest for your souls. For my yoke is easy, and my burden is light" (Matthew 11:28–30). Here is the never-ending promise of one who exists to give himself without limit in love and mercy and compassion to those most in need, most powerless, most lost or desperate or alone.

Why the Lord's heart? Because his heart is what *our* hearts are made for! The *Catechism of the Catholic Church* (2563) refers to the human heart as our "hidden center," the place to which we withdraw to be ourselves, where we really *live*. It is the locus of our decision making. It exists beyond the grasp of reason and remains deeper than all our psychic drives. The sanctuary of the heart is where we choose life or death.

But *left to ourselves, we cannot even know our own heart.* We need something more than ourselves in order to be in touch with our heart. Without the benefit of that "something," our hearts can become torturous.

Only God can fathom the human heart and know it fully. And so Jesus, in a supreme act of friendship, gives us his Sacred Heart so that we can know our own. The Sacred Heart of Jesus truly and completely corresponds with the longing of the human heart, satisfying its deepest need.

This notion of "heart" seems to be behind a moving insight of Fr. Hans Urs von Balthasar:

> God's love knows the depths. It lives in us, establishes itself within us as a center; we live from it; it fills and nourishes us; it draws us into its spell, clothing itself with us as a mantle and using our soul as its organ.... A loving fear grows within us, fear which again and more urgently forces us to our knees, into the dust of nothingness.... Thus do we live from God: he draws us mightily into his glowing core and robs us with his lordliness of every center that is not his own.... God claims us jealously; he wants us solely for himself and for his honor. But, laden with his love and living from his honor, he sends us back into the world.[84]

As Pope Benedict XVI says, "God's heart calls to our hearts, inviting us to come out of ourselves, to forsake our human certainties, to trust in him and, by following his example, to make ourselves a gift of unbounded love."[85] Our hearts are made for Something, and they cannot be tricked into settling for anything less than that Something—Someone!—for which we are made. Jesus blesses us with the gift of his Sacred Heart in order to provide an ingenious method to save us from the temptation of turning him into an abstraction, reducing him to his message or to his example.

The flame of Jesus's love set the young St. Thérèse of Lisieux on fire, moving her to profess that only Jesus can satisfy her soul, so boundless is her need of being loved by and loving Jesus. A poem of hers describes the fire in our own hearts:

"I need a heart burning with tenderness,
Who will be my support forever,
Who loves everything in me, even my weakness....
And who never leaves me day or night."
I could find no creature
Who could always love me and never die.
I must have a God who takes on my nature
And becomes my brother and is able to suffer!

You heard me, only Friend whom I love.
To ravish my heart, you became man.
...
O Heart of Jesus, treasure of tenderness,
You Yourself are my happiness, my only hope.
You who knew how to charm my tender youth,
Stay near me till the last night.
...
Ah! I know well, all our righteousness
Is worthless in your sight.
...
I hide myself in your Sacred Heart, Jesus.
I do not fear, my virtue is You![86]

Our Glorious Friends

The impulse of Jesus to share and to give himself lies at the heart of the glorious mystery of the Transfiguration (see Matthew 17:1–8; Mark 9:2–10; Luke 9:28–36)—an incomparable act of friendship. Jesus takes his three closest friends up a mountain, where he becomes transfigured before them, his face and clothes radiant, shining like the sun. It is as if, after spending so much time and going through so many powerful experiences with his friends, the Lord craves the chance to reveal to them something about him they have not yet perceived.

In commenting on the nature of friendship, St. Thomas Aquinas observes,

> Now, it is proper to friendship that a man reveals his secrets to his friend: because friendship unites their affections, and of two hearts makes one; and consequently when a man reveals something to his friend, he would seem not to have taken it out of his own heart. Hence our Lord said to his disciples (John 15:15): *I will now not call you servants... but I have called you friends, because all things whatsoever I have heard of my Father, I have made known to you.*[87]

On Mount Tabor, Christ the Friend is bursting to reveal the deepest secret of himself to his friends. He wants in every way to unite his affection with theirs, making their hearts one with his. "The essence of a perfect friendship," notes Msgr. Robert Hugh Benson (+1914) in his book *The Friendship of Christ*, "is that each friend reveals himself utterly to the other, flings aside his reserves, and shows himself for what he truly is."[88]

The fourteenth-century canon Walter Hilton, in *The Scale of Perfection*, revels in God's desire to display his secrets to us his friends:

> The lover of God is his friend, not because he has deserved to be, but because God in his merciful goodness has made him so by a very real pact. And so it is that he shows him his secrets as to a true friend who serves him through love and not through fear.[89]

The contemporary spiritual author Bishop Massimo Camisasca adds:

> The basis of friendship is a shared secret. A true relation-
> ship of friendship cannot last if it is only based on particular
> interests. There is always a divine secret among friends.…
> There is always a destiny towards which we run together, a
> total adventure that impassions and ignites each day of our
> lives. "I call you friends because I have told you everything."
> What is this "everything" that Christ said to his own, that
> he brought them? His communion with the Father. This is
> why the highest form of friendship man can live on earth is
> Christian communion, when it becomes the form of daily
> life.[90]

The burning tenderness of Jesus's Sacred Heart appears in the
Transfiguration as a near-blinding blaze. It draws us into the mystery
and to the very "heart" of that mystery, imparting to us a communion with the very Heart that causes Christ to shine.

Which leads to a second property of friendship, according to St.
Thomas Aquinas:

> The same union requires that the friend should share his
> belongings with him; because, since a man regards his friend
> as his other self, it follows that he will succor him as he
> would succor himself, by sharing his goods with him. Hence
> it is said to be a mark of friendship that a man in both will
> and deed should seek the good of his friend.[91]

The "looking glass" of the Transfiguration divulges the belongings that Jesus the Friend exults to share with us: the belongings of
belonging to him in the communion of love that the Son lives with the
Father. The heart that the Father has given to his Son with which to
love us, Jesus hands over to us so that we can love the Father.

To be a friend of Jesus means to receive this inestimable gift of his Sacred Heart and all it signifies. St. Margaret Mary Alacoque (+1690), a Visitation nun who received private revelations of the Sacred Heart and who is renowned for promoting devotion to the Sacred Heart, wrote:

> In everything and everywhere, I desire nothing but the accomplishment of the divine good pleasure, allowing the divine Heart of Jesus to will and desire in me and for me, just as he pleases. I am content to love him alone: whatever he wishes me to love, that he will love for me.... Everything that comes from the Sacred Heart is sweet. He changes everything into love.[92]

The confessor of Margaret Mary Alacoque, the Jesuit Father St. Claude de la Colombière (+1682), offers an additional word of encouragement:

> This Heart is still the same, always burning with love... always open so as to shower down graces and blessings upon us, always touched by our sorrows, always eager to impart its treasures to us and to give himself to us, always ready to receive us, to be our refuge, our dwelling place, and our heaven even in this world....[93] My Jesus, let me live in your heart and pour all my bitterness into it where it will be utterly consumed.[94]

THE COMMUNION OF FRIENDSHIP

We suffer in life due to conflict, alienation, and division in many forms. At times we find ourselves divided from other people, divided from God, and even divided within ourselves. Msgr. Giussani observed something our personal experience readily confirms: A person "gets off balance psychologically to the extent that he does not feel he belongs, that is, he is wanted, loved, fed, defended, and brought to fulfillment.... We are Christians because without Christ man begins to become less himself, to disappear."[95]

Just as we delight in harmony in music, we crave a similar, all-encompassing unity capable of permeating the whole of our life. The greatest possible joy is unity.

When Jesus commissions the twelve apostles, he sends them out two by two (Mark 6:7–12). Did you ever wonder why the Lord did that? Why not send each out on his own? That way the twelve could reach twice as many places.

But no, Jesus commissions them in pairs. For as the crowd listened to the one apostle who stood and preached, their eyes would shift to the companion apostle, seated to the side, waiting his turn. The people could perceive in the demeanor of that apostle, gazing in joy at his preaching colleague, the bond of love that cemented the two men. And that unity convinced the hearers of the reality of Jesus Christ. For it was a unity that no one could concoct or engineer. The crowds *saw* Jesus in the communion that the apostle pair witnessed to them.

And if you think about it, how many people in the world first came to "see" Jesus without ever being physically in the same location as he? They recognized Christ in the unity made evident by his disciples. They saw Jesus through that "sacrament" of unity long before they ever glimpsed him face-to-face. The people were attracted to a belonging, a unifying power that they experienced in the flesh.

Msgr. Guissani describes the power of the earliest communal gathering of the Church:

> We can see how the Church began: it literally allowed itself to "be seen" under Solomon's Portico, it proposed itself through the mere sight of it, through a first perception which can only be described as community....

That visible "we" was the first feature of the Church's face that an observer could have photographed....

Those who would gather under Solomon's Portico were the first sign. That emergent group of people presented themselves as people who, having the living presence of Christ among them, were the almost physiological continuity of that reality, bonded as they were to that living presence in the concreteness of daily, family life.[96]

The witness of the Christian community gathered under Solomon's Portico was "proof" of the resurrection of Jesus Christ. For here were gathered as one men and women, young and old, rich and poor, learned and uneducated, people of every race, every nation, every culture—united, beaming with joy and gladness, probably singing. What could bring about such remarkable unity among truly disparate, dissimilar people? Nothing that human ingenuity could engineer. Only God could effect this. Otherwise impossible community is one of Christ's first gifts of his resurrection.

The night before he died, Jesus prayed repeatedly for unity: "I... pray...that they may all be one; even as you, Father, are in me, and I in you, that they also may be in us,...that they may be one even as we are one, I in them and you in me" (John 17:20, 21–23).

Pope Benedict XVI comments on this prayer:

> The stated objective of Jesus' prayer for unity is precisely that through the unity of the disciples, the truth of his mission is made visible for men. Unity must be visible; it must be recognizable as something that does not exist elsewhere in the world; as something that is inexplicable on the basis of mankind's own efforts and that therefore makes visible the workings of a higher power. Through the humanly inexplicable unity of Jesus' disciples down the centuries, Jesus himself is vindicated. It can be seen that he is truly the

"Son." Hence God can be recognized as the creator of a unity that overcomes the world's inherent tendency toward fragmentation.

For this the Lord prayed: for a unity that can come into existence only from God and through Christ and yet is so concrete in its appearance that in it we are able to see God's power at work.[97]

In fact, the *Catechism of the Catholic Church* goes so far as to refer to the communal gathering of the Church as "God's reaction to the chaos provoked by sin" (CCC, 761). This great gift of palpable unity, which in so many ways inaugurated the Church, would become the world's lasting, transforming gift in the Eucharist.

We understand the indispensability of such unity when we ponder what life would be like without it. Msgr. Giussani writes:

> Whether or not we are aware of it, the way in which we feel, see, and judge comes from what we belong to…. If man belonged to nothing, then he would be nothing…. If there weren't the awareness of a belonging, then he would be faced with his own nothingness….
>
> The human being exists because he is continually possessed. And when he recognizes this, then he breathes fully, feels at peace, glad.[98]

A COMMUNION OF FRIENDS

The great painter Vincent Van Gogh suffered from overwhelming bouts of self-persecution and depression. Yet in a July 1880 letter to his brother, Theo, Van Gogh named the antidote:

> Dear Theo,
> A caged bird in spring…is well aware that there is something to be done, but he is unable to do it…. He says to himself,

"The others are building their nest and hatching their young and bringing them up," and then he bangs his head against the bars of the cage. But the cage does not give way, and the bird is maddened by pain....

People are often unable to do anything, imprisoned as they are in I don't know what kind of terrible, terrible, oh such terrible cage....

You cannot always tell what keeps you confined, what immures you, what seems to bury you, and yet you can feel those elusive bars, railings, walls.... And then one asks: "My God! will it be for long, will it be for ever, will it be for eternity?

Do you know what makes the prison disappear? Every deep, genuine affection. Being friends, being brothers, loving, that is what opens the prison, with supreme power, by some magic force. Without these one stays dead....[99]

The great North American missionary and martyr St. Isaac Jogues (+1646) was taken prisoner by a warring Native American tribe. The captors stripped Fr. Jogues of his black robe, dragged him to where his coprisoners—fellow French missioners and Huron converts—were huddled. When one of them began to tie leather thongs around his ankles. Fr. Jogues protested:

No, no. You don't need to bind me. These French and Hurons whom you have taken, they are the bonds that will keep me captive. I won't leave them till death. I will follow them everywhere. You can be assured of my person as long as any one of them remains among you as a prisoner.[100]

With that the captors left Isaac Jogues untethered, so impressed were they by his invisible bonds of belonging.

This experience of St. Isaac Jogues verifies something the medieval Pseudo-Hugh of St. Victor once explained: The devil fears nothing more than unity in charity. If we distribute everything we own for God, the devil does not fear this, because he himself does not own anything. If we fast he is not afraid, because he does not take food. And if we keep vigil, he feels no terror, because he does not sleep. But if we are united in charity, he is afraid of this, and immensely so. Because by our lived union of charity we safeguard on earth what he disdained to preserve in heaven.

Therefore the Church is described as terrible, like an army in orderly array. Because just as enemies are afraid when they see the ranks of an army line up and group together for war, so clearly the devil is frightened when he sees spiritual people, equipped with the weapons of virtue, living in harmonious unity.[101]

What terrifies hell is *communion*. Communion, wrote Msgr. Giussani, "is an inner dimension at the source of our thoughts and actions."[102] The belonging of community is having other key people of our life "inside us." We can have communion only if we give ourselves to something beyond ourselves. That communion becomes the defining aspect of our life.

The Carthusian Dom Augustin Guillerand (+1945), in reflecting on the meaning of community, wrote:

> When two souls are united, they do not lie side by side like two bodies; they are really each in the other. And this is the principle of all love union, and in particular of that friendship which is the highest form of that union. Two friends become one, because their minds and their hearts are in perfect harmony, in the worship of the same truth and in the love of the same good. That community of love—note the word "community" which means "common-unity" and is very significant—increases our life twofold, and makes our

being greater with all the greatness of the life of the one we love. That is how, when we love God and when we enter into these relations of friendship with him, our life takes on a wideness which is measureless, and becomes eternal life.[103]

THE IRRESISTIBLE ATTRACTION OF GOD'S FRIENDSHIP

One scene in the breathtaking film *Of Gods and Men* shows a Muslim girl asking a Trappist monk what falling in love is like. He is one of a community of monks who have elected to stay in their monastery in Tibhirine, Algeria, despite recent murderous terrorist activity that has been traumatizing the entire region. Soon these very monks will be abducted in the dead of night and martyred.

The Trappist, Brother Luc, gives a most amazing answer to the girl's question: "There's something inside you that comes alive, the presence of someone. It's irrepressible and makes your heart beat faster. It's an attraction, a desire." When the girl asks Luc if he has even been in love, he answers, "Yes, several times. And then I encountered another love, even greater. And I answered that love."[104]

St. Claude de la Colombière knows this Greater Love:

Jesus, you are my only true and real friend. You share all my sorrows and take them upon yourself, knowing how to turn them to my good. You listen to me kindly when I tell you of my difficulties, and you never fail to lighten them. Wherever I go I always find you; you never leave me, and if I am obliged to go away, I find you waiting for me.

You are never weary of listening to me, and you never cease to do me good. I am sure of being loved if I love you. You have no need of me or of my goods, and you do not deprive yourself by giving me of your riches. However wretched I am, no one nobler or more clever or even more holy can rob me of your friendship; and death which separates us from

all other friends will only unite me to you. All the accidents
of age or of fortune will never detach you from me; on the
contrary, I shall never enjoy you more fully and you will
never be so close to me as when everything goes against me.
You bear with my defects with tender patience; even my infi-
delities and ingratitude do not wound you in such a way that
you are not always ready to return to me when I call upon
you.[105]

A modern proponent of St. Claude's Jesuit charism expresses a
similar ardor:

Nothing is more practical than
finding God, than
falling in Love
in a quite absolute, final way.
What you are in love with,
what seizes your imagination, will affect everything.
It will decide
what will get you out of bed in the morning,
what you do with your evenings,
how you spend your weekends,
what you read, whom you know,
what breaks your heart,
and what amazes you with joy and gratitude.
Fall in Love, stay in love,
and it will decide everything.[106]

We may attempt to resist God's friendship at first. But the winning
attraction of the love of God has the power to sweep us away, as
Msgr. Robert Hugh Benson attests:

Let me tell you how I made His acquaintance.

I had heard much of Him, but took no heed.

He sent daily gifts and presents, but I never thanked Him.

He often seemed to want my friendship, but I remained cold.

I was homeless, and wretched, and starving and in peril every hour; and He offered me shelter and comfort and food and safety; but I was ungrateful still.

At last He crossed my path and with tears in His eyes He besought me saying, Come and abide with me.

Let me tell you how He treats me now.

He supplies all my wants.

He gives me more than I dare ask.

He anticipates my every need.

He begs me to ask for more.

He never reminds me of my past ingratitude.

He never rebukes me for my past follies.

Let me tell you further what I think of Him.

He is as good as He is great.

His love is as ardent as it is true.

He is as lavish of His promises as He is faithful in keeping them.

He is as jealous of my love as He is deserving of it.

I am in all things His debtor, but He bids me call Him Friend.[107]

The gift of divine friendship in Jesus moves us to want to pray with Blessed Charles de Foucauld:

Father,

I abandon myself into your hands; do with me what you will.

Whatever you may do, I thank you;
I am ready for all, I accept all.
Let only your will be done in me, and in all your creatures.
I wish no more than this, O Lord.

Into your hands I commend my soul;
I offer it to you
with all the love of my heart,
for I love you, Lord,
and so need to give myself,
to surrender myself into your hands,
without reserve,
and with boundless confidence,
for you are my Father.[108]

CHAPTER FOUR

THE LOVE THAT IS MERCY

In the bottomless depths of mercy, pardon, and love of the heart of Jesus, I drown sin, hatred, and godlessness. Into his redeeming, sanctifying, and divine blood I plunge guilty, ungrateful, and blind souls. I hide fearful, timid, and untrusting souls in his sacred wounds. I submerge cold, obdurate, and rebellious hearts in the limitless ocean of his tenderness.[109]

—SERVANT OF GOD MARTHE ROBIN

Which one of us has not, at some point in time, felt like the lost sheep (see Luke 15:3–7)—languishing in a plight of our own making, waiting for a compassionate arm to lift us to safety? Or like the woman caught in adultery (John 8:2–11), who despite damning guilt, pines to hear Mercy's soothing voice, *Has no one condemned you? Neither do I condemn you.* Or the tax collector (Luke 18:9–14), overwhelmed by his own corruption and evil, who nonetheless flings himself in humility before the Mystery begging, *God, be merciful to me a sinner!* Or like the prodigal son (Luke 15:11–32), who after running through every available resource of his life, comes to his senses at last with the resolve, *I will arise and go to my Father.*

As the contemporary Christian singer Audrey Assad prays in her moving song "Show Me":

Bind up these broken bones
Mercy bend and breathe me back to life.[110]

THE MIRACLE OF MERCY

St. Faustina Kowalska (+1938), from whose writings the Church has received the Chaplet of Divine Mercy, records these haunting words in her famous diary: "Humanity will never find peace until it turns with trust to Divine Mercy."[111]

Why mercy?

To experience mercy is to be loved when we deserve love the least. In mercy we are loved not because of our own goodness but because of the goodness of another. Mercy is the creative love of God that gives itself freely beyond all demands, all rights, and all measures.

St. John Paul II, early in his pontificate, turned the world's attention to divine mercy in his astonishing encyclical *Dives in Misericordia* ("Rich in Mercy"). The Holy Father extols mercy as that love that "is able to reach down...to every human misery.... When this happens, the person who is the object of mercy...feel[s]...found again and restored to value." He speaks of mercy as "an indispensable dimension of love; it is as it were love's second name and, at the same time, the specific manner in which love is revealed and effected." The truest and proper aspect of mercy consists in its power to recover, promote, and draw good from all forms of evil existing in us and in the world.[112]

Is this transformative power of mercy real?

In 1957 a young Frenchman by the name of Jacques Fesch was sentenced to death for murdering a police officer during a foiled robbery attempt. Jacques was a young man of privilege who had squandered his youth in a dissolute lifestyle. No amount of self-indulgence managed to sate him, though, and he concocted a fanciful plan to sail away to the South Pacific, where he would make a new life for himself in the sun. However, when his parents refused to finance a boat he aimed to buy, Jacques instead conceived a scheme to rob a Parisian moneychanger. It failed. Fleeing the crime scene, Jacques fired his gun, killing a pursuing policeman, Jean Vergne.

Jacques was convicted of murder and sentenced to execution. After some months in prison, he experienced a profound conversion to the faith. He recounts it in his journal:

> I was in bed, eyes open, really suffering for the first time in my life.... It was then that a cry burst from my breast, an appeal for help—My God!—and instantly, like a violent wind which passes over without anyone knowing where it comes from, the spirit of the Lord seized me by the throat.
>
> I had an impression of infinite power and kindness and, from that moment onward, I believed with an unshakeable conviction that has never left me.[113]

The testimony of Jacques Fesch (whose cause for canonization has been introduced!) verifies something that Pope Francis said when he was Cardinal Bergoglio:

> Only someone who has encountered mercy, who has been caressed by the tenderness of mercy, is happy and comfortable with the Lord....
>
> In front of this merciful embrace...we feel a real desire to respond, to change, to correspond; a new morality arises....
>
> And if someone starts to ask for it, then he begins to change.... There from the depths of my being, something attracts me toward Someone who looked for me first, is waiting for me first.[114]

As St. Paul declares (reflecting no doubt on his own personal experience), "But God, who is rich in mercy, out of the great love with which he loved us, even when we were dead through our trespasses, made us alive together with Christ" (Ephesians 2:4–5).

So often we feel oppressed by the nothingness (the nihilism) of life. Mercy transfigures that. The quality of mercy, notes St. Thomas Aquinas, consists in bringing a thing out of nonbeing into being.[115] It brings *us* out of our non-being into being.

The miracle of mercy appeals to our freedom, beckoning us to respond. As Msgr. Giussani writes:

> It is now our turn to make it our self, acting from within this mercy, failing which we shall betray our deepest nature....
>
> I am no longer I; my name is the name of Christ who is mercy.... All that matters is that mercy has taken you for ever, from the very origin of your existence. Mercy called to you, because mercy loved you.[116]

Mercy Encounters Peter

One of the most powerful manifestations of mercy of all time stems from one of the most appalling acts of betrayal. As Christ is led off to his passion, the apostle Peter three times denies knowing Jesus (Matthew 26:69–75). Peter's cowardice thankfully leads to contrition and not to despair...as it did for Judas Iscariot.

Perhaps what saves Peter from Judas's fate is an earlier episode of presumption also trumped by Christ's mercy. After a long, unproductive night of fishing, Jesus stepped into Simon Peter's boat and issued this command: "Put out into the deep and let down your nets for a catch" (Luke 5:4). Peter, the "expert" fisherman, maybe both tired from his labors and put out by this "meddling," petulantly replied, "Master, we toiled all night and took nothing!" (Luke 5:5). But he complied with Christ's word nonetheless, and the result was a mountainous haul that threatened to sink *two* boats.

The greatest miracle of the day was not the Lord's ability to produce fish where there had been none, nor was it the spectacular, incalculable quantity of the catch. The greatest miracle of the day was that

Mercy preferred to stay with a despondent Peter who saw his sins and what his sins deserved: "Depart from me, for I am a sinful man, O Lord" (Luke 5:8). Mercy claimed Simon Peter that day.

It is by a fire that Peter's denial of Christ occurs (see Luke 22:55), and it is by a fire that Peter's reinstating, threefold confession also takes place (John 21:9, 15–19). After Peter the Rock hits rock bottom in his denial of Jesus, he discovers something undeniable about himself: His love for Jesus exceeds the enormity of his evil.

The Lord's question, posed three times—*Do you love me?*—probes Peter at a depth of self he perhaps never experienced before. In the face of his atrocious sins, the question almost comes off as mockery. *Of* course *I don't love you; just look at my conduct toward you! Isn't that answer enough?* But maybe it is more than just the words that arrest Peter and make him consider the question seriously.

You may know Dr. Eben Alexander's amazing book *Proof of Heaven*. It recounts his otherworldly experiences when he was stricken by a seven-day coma. In particular it contains an account of meeting a young woman who accompanied him for most of his journey. Among many remarkable things about the young woman, what struck him particularly was her *gaze*.

> She looked at me with a look that, if you saw it for a few moments, would make your whole life up to that point worth living, no matter what had happened in it so far.... It was something higher, holding all...other kinds of love within itself while at the same time being much bigger than all of them.[117]

Through that look of love, the woman communicated a three-part message to Alexander: You are loved and cherished, dearly, forever; you have nothing to fear; there is nothing you can do wrong. Maybe something similar transpires in Peter through the gaze of love with which Jesus presents his question.

Even more, Peter remembers that long ago command of Christ in his life—*Put out into the deep!*—and he puts out into the deep of himself. There he discovers he is not alone. Someone is waiting for him in those depths, in that darkness. In the depths of himself Peter comes face-to-face with the fact that his sin does not define him. The deepest truth about Peter is that he *is* a relationship with the Mystery that has not stopped stepping into his life ever since stepping into his boat. Peter is part of a *belonging*. Even sin and evil cannot erase that.

Fr. Julián Carrón comments:

> Facing his evil, Peter did not experience what was missing. The living presence of Jesus, in the superabundance of mercy, imposed itself on his remorse. This is what becomes more powerful than any evil; the grandeur of his living presence becomes more imposing than any nihilism, through the superabundance of his presence....[118]
>
> When I have done something very bad, so bad that I am scandalized at myself, what defines me in that moment? Christ's embrace of me in baptism, that not even my wrong can undo.... Nothing I can do can change Christ's attitude towards me.... When I am reduced to nothing, to the point that I am ashamed to look at myself, in that moment I can say "What defines me?" This embrace of Christ, this being taken hold of by Christ, which remains after this wrong I have done.[119]

What at first may have seemed like an interrogation is in fact the Lord's method of raising Simon Peter back to life, in much the same way he did his other dead friend, Lazarus (see John 11:1–45). By his thrice-repeated question, Christ commands: *Peter, come forth! Leave*

behind the stink of your denial, the tomb of your betrayal. In the
embrace of your love for me, be unbound and set free. Roll away the
stone of regret! You are Rock! On this Rock I will build my Church.
Feed my sheep.

Peter finds himself loved by a Love that surpasses his reprehensible
shame and its otherwise irreversible trauma. Just as once a tumul-
tuous storm at sea moved Peter to beg Christ for the impossible—
"Lord, if it is you, bid me come to you on the water" (Matthew
14:28)—so now Peter is goaded by the tempestuous waves of his own
weeping. He makes his *yes* to resurrected Mercy by daring to walk
across the waters of his own tears.

The risen Christ, in his great mercy, responds by giving Peter a new
birth "to a living hope through the resurrection of Jesus Christ from
the dead" (1 Peter 1:3). Peter's feelings of being convicted turn glori-
ously into lasting conviction: *You know that I love you.* St. Thomas
Aquinas observes: "Christ says, *Do you love me more than these*
because the more Peter loves the better he is."[120]

French Bishop Jacques-Benigne Bossuet (+1704) remarks on the
recreative power of the love that is mercy:

> In the whole teaching of the Gospels there is nothing more
> touching than God's gentle and loving way of treating His
> reconciled enemies.... He is not satisfied with blotting out
> our stains and washing away our filth.... In fact, He receives
> penitent sinners back with so much love that innocence itself
> might almost be said to have cause for complaint—or at
> least for some jealousy—at the sight of it....
>
> Our Lord not only never shows contempt for sinners by
> banishing them from His presence, but actually calls them
> to the highest offices in His kingdom. He entrusts the charge
> of His flock to a Peter who has denied Him; He puts the
> publican Matthew at the head of the Evangelists; and makes

Paul, the chief of persecutors, into the first of preachers—not the just and innocent, but the converted sinners, have the first places.[121]

Mercy Encounters Paul

Speaking of St. Paul, he is the author of the timeless, unparalleled hymn to charity in 1 Corinthians 13. But if we reflect for a moment, we realize that there is something very strange about this.

Who was Saul of Tarsus before he met Jesus Christ on the road to Damascus? He was an atrociously evil man. Saul's fanatical efforts as he "persecuted the Church of God" (1 Corinthians 15:9) went beyond anything anyone can imagine. The Acts of the Apostles describes Saul as one who was "breathing threats and murder against the disciples of the Lord" (Acts 9:1). Paul accuses himself of being an accomplice in the murder of the martyr St. Stephen (see Acts 8:1; 22:20). He admits, "In raging fury against [the disciples of Christ], I persecuted them even to foreign cities" (Acts 26:11). He is described as one who "made havoc...of those who called on [Jesus's] name" (Acts 9:21).

Paul confesses to Jesus himself, "I imprisoned and beat those who believed in you" (Acts 22:19). He says, "I persecuted the Church of God violently and tried to destroy it" (Galatians 1:13). He sums up his life with these words: "Christ Jesus came into the world to save sinners. And I am the foremost of sinners" (1 Timothy 1:15).

In his book *Paul of Tarsus*, Msgr. Joseph Holzner captures Saul's dilemma (which we can verify in our own experience):

> Saul traveled through sin and darkness before he found Christ.... When a man feels the burden of guilt on his soul, he tries hard to justify himself before his own conscience and before others by increasing his false zeal, and thus he sinks yet deeper into evil.[122]

Pope Benedict XVI confirms this insight: "Paul...understood that...
he had sought to build up himself and his own justice, and that with
all this justice he had lived for himself."[123]

Looking at his history from another angle, we can say this: Paul was
a person whose whole life was dedicated to exterminating systemati-
cally an entire category of human beings. Does that remind you of
anyone? And yet this notoriously violent and evil man, who was at
one time the world's foremost, unrivaled, expert hater, has become
for all time the unsurpassed, supreme, definitive authority on love.
How did *that* ever happen?

Clearly, no one arrives at such a knowledge of love by reading
about it in a book. There is only one explanation for Saul's certainty
about love: He encountered it personally. Mercy came and claimed
Saul of Tarsus.

The proof of this is the way Paul introduces his classic hymn to
charity: "I will show you a still more excellent way" (1 Corinthians
12:31). He doesn't say that he will show us a still more excellent
theory, or principle, or idea, or concept, or model, or plan, or notion,
or image, or doctrine, or philosophy, or metaphor, or anything else.
He says, "I will show you a still more excellent *way*."

The Greek word used there for "way" is *hodos* (the root of the
word *method*). A *hodos* is a path, a trail, a route, a physical road,
that we follow in order to get somewhere. What is the way that
Paul wants to show us? Remember: It is not something figurative
or symbolic or poetic but rather an actual, concrete, real-life *hodos*.
What is it? *The road to Damascus!*

Paul always lived the *memory* of what took place in him on the
road to Damascus (see Acts 9:1–9)—"memory" meaning a rehap-
pening of an event. In the miraculous encounter with Jesus Christ on
that road, Paul experienced a profound grace of mercy. It was this

personal encounter with Mercy-made-flesh that endowed Paul with the singular, magisterial authority to speak about love.

Without doubt, Paul every day returned spiritually to the road to Damascus and relived the encounter with the Way, the Truth, the Life, Jesus Christ (see John 14:6). In his great hymn to charity, St. Paul wants to put us on that road and into that encounter with Jesus that never ends. For being Christian, the encyclical *God Is Love* teaches us, "is not the result of an ethical choice or a lofty idea, but the encounter with an event, a person, which gives life a new horizon and a decisive direction."[124] Or to rephrase it in Paul's language, "'Knowledge' puffs up, but love builds up" (1 Corinthians 8:1).

Love, charity, is a road! Which moves St. Anselm to pray, "Make me...taste by love that which I taste by knowledge; to perceive by affection what I perceive by understanding."[125]

Paul's hymn to charity brings us into the heart of that encounter with Christ, giving our life the same new horizon and decisive direction that permanently transformed his. St. Paul knew what St. John knew: "God is love" (1 John 4:16). Paul can assert, "Love is patient and kind" (1 Corinthians 13:4), because it was God's patient, kind love that came and converted him on the road to Damascus. Up until that moment, Paul was the perfect antithesis of patience and kindness: he was hideously intolerant and cruel. The proof of the reality of Love is how that it transfigured the agitated, brutal Saul of Tarsus into a sublimely kind and patient man.

"Love is not jealous or boastful" (1 Corinthians 13:4). Paul can make this claim based on his former state of being consumed by such vices. No lesson or lecture can persuade a narcissist to leave off arrogant, envious, self-serving ways. But when Love came and looked him in the eye, jealousy and egoism melted away. Paul tasted the joy of loving Love instead of adulating vanity. It led him later to proclaim, "Let him who boasts, boast of the Lord" (1 Corinthians 1:31).

"Love does not insist on its own way" (1 Corinthians 13:5). Love knows it will win; it will triumph over any darkness, any resistance. How personally struck was Paul by a truth of the Gospel he would ultimately teach: "But God...out of the great love with which he loved us, even when we were dead through our trespasses, made us alive together with Christ" (Ephesians 2:4–5). "God shows his love for us in that while we were yet sinners Christ died for us" (Romans 5:8). The verification of this quality of love is the fact that Paul embodies it. As he explains to the Corinthians, "When reviled, we bless; when persecuted, we endure; when slandered, we try to conciliate" (1 Corinthians 4:12–13).

Love "is not irritable or resentful; it does not rejoice at wrong" (1 Corinthians 13:5–6). Paul can testify to this because Love has liberated him from his own crippling irritability, resentfulness, and morose delectation.

"Love bears all things, believes all things, hopes all things, endures all things" (1 Corinthians 13:7). And so now also does Paul, because Love has made him that way, purging and purifying even the most minute aspects of his personality. And nothing less than Love could accomplish such a miracle.

Paul must have loved the Gospel stories he was taught in the course of his catechesis about the woman at the well, the adulterous woman, the Pharisee and the tax collector in the Temple, but especially the prodigal son. When Paul heard that parable, he must have been convinced that it was about himself! We can *feel* Paul's heart in his letter to the Colossians, "[God] has delivered us from the dominion of darkness" (Colossians 1:13).

Msgr. Joseph Holzner imagines a conversation between the apostles Peter and Paul. He has Paul say:

Cephas, the most amazing thing about all this is the miracle of his love. That the Master should love me, that he should forgive me, reveal himself to me, to me who persecuted him, who attacked the members of his mystical body, loaded them with chains and put them to death, that is incomprehensible.[126]

St. John Chrysostom preaches about how divine charity transformed the apostle Paul:

The most important thing of all to him…was that he knew himself to be loved by Christ. Enjoying this love, he considered himself happier than anyone else; were he without it, it would be no satisfaction to be the friend of principalities and powers. He preferred to be thus loved and be the least of all, or even to be among the damned, than to be without that love and be among the great and honored.[127]

That love was contagious. There's a bizarre story in Acts 16 (verses 25–34) about Paul being thrown in prison with Silas. According to the account, at around midnight a severe earthquake shook the foundations of the jail. All the doors flew open, and the chains of all the prisoners came loose. When the jailer saw this, he pulled out his sword so as to kill himself. But Paul shouted out to him, "Do no harm to yourself, for we are all here."

The odd thing is: Why didn't Paul escape when the jail doors flew open? Because Paul was not interested in "release"; he was interested in *freedom*. As he says in the letter to the Galatians, "For freedom Christ has set us free" (Galatians 5:1).

The jailer saw in Paul a freedom that no prison could ever confine or constrict. And it made him want it for himself. So much so that later that jailer, along with his entire family, were converted. And it was all because of the fact that Paul decided to stay in jail even when given a miraculous way out. What made Paul stay in that jail? Love. And that is what made the jailer want to stay with Paul.

Charity is a road; charity is friendship; charity is a road that leads to friendship. St. Fulgentius of Ruspe (+533) marvels at the way Saul became the favored friend of one he had conspired to murder:

> Strengthened by the power of [God's] love, [Stephen] overcame the raging cruelty of Saul and won his persecutor on earth as his companion in heaven....
>
> Now at last, Paul rejoices with Stephen, with Stephen he delights in the glory of Christ, with Stephen he exalts, with Stephen he reigns. Stephen went first, slain by the stones thrown by Paul, but Paul followed after, helped by the prayer of Stephen. This, surely, is the true life, my brothers, a life in which Paul feels no shame because of Stephen's death, and Stephen delights in Paul's companionship, for love fills them both with joy. It was Stephen's love that prevailed over the cruelty of the mob, and it was Paul's love that covered the multitude of his sins; it was love that won for both of them the kingdom of heaven.
>
> Love, indeed, is the source of all good things; it is an impregnable defense, and the way that leads to heaven. He who walks in love can neither go astray nor be afraid: love guides him, protects him, and brings him to his journey's end.[128]

LIVING IN MERCY

As I reflect upon my own experience, I realize that much of my former life was caught up in a malaise identified by the fifth-century ascetic St. Diadochus of Photiki: "Very few [people] can accurately recognize all their own faults; indeed, only those can do this whose intellect is never torn away from the remembrance of God."[129]

Having to recognize our own sins may well be the most repellent—
if not the most terrifying—project in life. Which is why God himself,
in dialogue with St. Catherine of Siena, reveals this instruction:

> I do not want [the soul] to...think about her sins either in
> general or specifically without calling to mind the blood [of
> Christ] and the greatness of my mercy. Otherwise she will be
> confounded.[130]

> I grant [the] knowledge [of sin] not to lead [people] to
> despair but to lead them to perfect self-knowledge and hope-
> filled shame over their sinfulness so that they may atone for
> their sins with discerning shame and placate my wrath by
> humbly asking for mercy.[131]

Keeping our intellect attuned to remembrance of God calls for delib-
erate mindfulness of the great mercy of Jesus. Let us meditate on his
sacred passion *before* we think about our sins.

This dynamic springs to life in a famous scene from Victor Hugo's
Les Miserables. Jean Valjean, recently released from nineteen years
of imprisonment for stealing a loaf of bread, in the dark of night
absconds with the silverware of the kindly and compassionate bishop
who has shown him hospitality. The police apprehend the thief and
bring him back to the bishop so that he can accuse man. Instead the
bishop says to Valjean:

> Ah! here you are!... I am glad to see you. Well, but how is
> this? I gave you the candlesticks too, which are of silver like
> the rest, and for which you can certainly get two hundred
> francs. Why did you not carry them away with your forks
> and spoons?[132]

That tangible experience of mercy gave this formerly seething, cynical,
angry, resentful man the ability to look at his own sins, and in that

knowledge to repent and be permanently converted. Jean Valjean himself becomes a man of heroic charity, generosity, self-sacrifice, and benevolence.

Paul Claudel (+1955) captured the attractive force of divine mercy:

> [Jesus] knows the sweetest words of love, He murmurs them into the ears of our poor ravished souls....
>
> His whole campaign up to the very end is a profusion of good deeds.... He gives sight to the blind and hearing to the deaf, He purifies the lepers, He drives out unclean spirits... but more wonderful still, He forgives sins! He knows that we cannot help loving someone who is good to us, and if it is through God that this good is done, well, perhaps we will begin to love God a little and to obey Him, for it is clear and evident that in this way lies salvation.[133]

St. Alphonsus Liguori says something similar: "Since God knew that man is enticed by favors, he wished to bind him to his love by means of his gifts."[134]

Only being bowled over by the greatness of God's mercy propels us past the resistance to face our sins. The abbot St. Dorotheus of Gaza offered uncannily relevant counsel in the sixth century:

> The reason for all disturbance, if we look to its roots, is that no one finds fault with himself.
>
> This is the source of all annoyance and distress. This is why we sometimes have no rest....
>
> In our laziness and desire for rest, we hope or believe that we have entered upon a straight path when we are impatient with everyone, and yet cannot bear to blame ourselves.
>
> This is the way we are. It does not matter how many virtues a man may have, even if they are beyond number and limit. If he has turned from the path of self-accusation,

he will never find peace. He will always be troubled himself, or else he will be a source of trouble for others and all his labors will be wasted.[135]

In the succinct words of the great Catholic author George Bernanos, "Sin makes us live at the surface of ourselves. We will again go back into ourselves only to die, and it's there He awaits us."[136]

We need help to be able to die to ourselves and die to sin. For me that grace was granted through the fatherly care of a holy priest (to whom I will be grateful for the rest of my life). We are not meant to face our wretchedness alone. What crucifies Christ is our sins, and God always sends us a Simon of Cyrene (Luke 23:26) to help us carry that cross. As the poet Rainer Maria Rilke (+1926) recognized so well, "It's here in all the pieces of my shame that I find myself again."[137] The presence of a holy companion helps us confront that shame, not with dread but with confidence.

For years I had dismissed my sins, denied my sins, rationalized my sins, made excuses for them, tried to bargain my way out of them—in short, I was blackmailed by my sins. It was this holy priest who introduced me to St. Thérèse of Lisieux, the incandescent young Carmelite nun who was to be my primary spiritual physician long before becoming a doctor of the Church. She wrote with uncanny, impervious certainty about the mercy of God:

> We must consent to remain always poor and without strength, and this is the difficulty.... Let us love our little-ness, let us love to feel nothing, then we shall be poor in spirit, and Jesus will come to look for us, and *however far* we may be, He will transform us in flames of love.[138]

The scintillating simplicity of this doctrine seemed way too good to be true. I always had presumed that my littleness, my nothingness, was the thing God liked about me the least. Even more, I presumed it was the very source of all my problems. But a compelling, paradoxical logic came shining through Thérèse's breakthrough spiritual counsel:

> If God wants you to be as weak and powerless as a child, do you think your merit will be any less for that? Resign yourself, then, to stumbling at every step, to falling even, and to being weak in carrying your cross. Love your powerlessness, and your soul will benefit more from it than if, aided by grace, you were to behave with enthusiastic heroism—and fill your soul with self-satisfaction.[139]

Why is this so reasonable? Because it fulfills a plea of the psalms that has never ceased to sound through the centuries: "Be still, and know that I am God" (Psalm 46:10). And how are we to "know" God? The way that the Savior of the world personally, painstakingly reveals: *I have not come to call the well but the sick* (see Mark 2:17).

Faith and confidence in her Savior moved Thérèse to pray:

> I expect each day to discover new imperfections in myself....
>
> I am simply resigned to see myself always imperfect—and in this I find my joy....
>
> My own folly is this: to trust that your love will accept me....
>
> I am only a child, powerless and weak, and yet it is my weakness that gives me the boldness of offering myself as a victim of your love, O Jesus![140]

How many of us twist ourselves into spiritual knots, presupposing that God demands something from us we do not have. We yearn for the perfection of holiness, but our defects, weaknesses, flaws, and faults seem to set up an impassable roadblock...or so we falsely think. We hold back from going to God, weighed down with myriad imperfections that we mistakenly presume disqualify us from the pursuit of sanctity.

This conflicts us. We want God; we want to be like God; yet we see how unlike God we are. And that knowledge makes us stay away; it makes us sad. The evil one distorts our reluctance to go to God so that it actually seems like *a pious thing*.

Yet the truth of the Gospel is that the more God enables us to see and admit our unworthiness and misery, the more he supplies us with the grace we need to cleave to him. When we come to Jesus in the knowledge of our evil—without trying to fix it on our own or making excuses for it—we glorify him the most, because it is in that profound act of faith that we concretely depend on him for everything.

The little child who falls and scrapes his knee doesn't delay, contemplating some self-cure. He leaps up and runs into the arms of his mother or father. This is what it means to live in mercy.

Pope Benedict XVI once said, citing Augustine, "World history...is a struggle between two kinds of love: self-love to the point of hatred for God, and love of God to the point of self-renunciation."[141] The self-renunciation that makes way for true, strong love of God entails letting God love us right now, in these given circumstances, just the way we are. Our only misgivings should be about not disposing ourselves to receive God's love moment by moment.

St. Thérèse puts it perfectly: "To please Jesus, to delight his heart, one has only to love him, without looking at one's self."[142] "What pleases Jesus is to see me love my lowliness and poverty, to see the blind hope I have in his mercy."[143]

MERCY'S WONDER

St. Augustine counsels us with words that are as liberating as they are wise: "Let us never assume that if we live good lives we will be without sin; our lives should be praised only when we continue to beg for pardon."[144] For as Msgr. Giussani comments:

Approaching the Mystery requires only one thing: the awareness of our ineptitude, which is more than nothingness; of our basic incapacity and our continuous betrayal.[145]

In the long run, whoever recognizes himself as a sinner, with all the pain involved—the mark of intensity of one's desire—must surely be on the road to true self-realization as a real human being, one who belongs to Christ.[146]

Translated into practical terms, to live mercy means that we go to sacramental confession often and regularly—a nonnegotiable in the life of faith.

The wonder of the love that is mercy rings in the incomparable prayer of Lieutenant Andre Zirnheld (+1942) of Britain's Special Air Service, who was killed in action during the Second World War:

I bring this prayer to You, Lord,
For You alone can give
What one cannot demand from oneself.

Give me, Lord, what you have left over,
Give me what no one ever asks of You.

I don't ask You for rest,
Or quiet,
Whether of soul or body;
I don't ask You for wealth,
Nor for success, nor even health perhaps.

That sort of thing You get asked for so much
That You can't have any of it left.

Give me, Lord, what You have left over,
Give me what no one wants from You.

I want insecurity, strife,
And I want You to give me these
Once and for all.

So that I can be sure of having them always,
Since I shall not always have the courage
To ask You for them.

Give me, Lord, what You have left over,
Give me what others want nothing to do with.

But give me courage too,
And strength and faith;
For You alone can give
What one cannot demand from oneself.[147]

CHAPTER FIVE

THE INNER SIDE OF LOVE: SUFFERING

Suffering is a sign—a sign that we have come so close to Jesus on the cross, that he can kiss us, show that he is in love with us by giving us an opportunity to share in his Passion.[148]
—BLESSED TERESA OF CALCUTTA

The moment we start to love, the specter of suffering arises. Why? Because to love you means I never want to lose you. Losing you would bring on unimaginable suffering. But the only way to avert the suffering of loss would be not to love you in the first place. Not an option—that's even less bearable. Thus there is an unavoidable, intrinsic link between love and suffering.

Cardinal Joseph Ratzinger spoke about this connection in an interview:

> Pain is part of being human. Anyone who really wanted to get rid of suffering would have to get rid of love before anything else, because there can be no love without suffering, because it always demands an element of self-sacrifice, because, given temperamental differences and the drama of situations, it will always bring with it renunciation and pain.[149]

Later as pope, in his encyclical on hope, Benedict XVI added :

> In the end, even the "yes" to love is a source of suffering, because love always requires expropriations of my "I," in which I allow myself to be pruned and wounded. Love

simply cannot exist without this painful renunciation of myself.[150]

DISCOVERY THROUGH SUFFERING

Suffering is overwhelming. When it strikes we feel done for. We presume there's no option but to succumb.

But the poet Gertrude von Le Fort (+1971) sees suffering another way. She writes, "I have gone down to the waters of despair, / but they are not deeper than my own heart."[151] Even when engulfed in life's most harrowing misery, we sense Something Greater.

"One cannot speak of real misery," notes Dominican Fr. Dominique Barthelemy (+2002), "until it has reached the stage where man forgets the possibility of liberation."[152] But the possibility of liberation remains *always there*. Suffering draws us to a deeper depth of remembering. A wondrous power of the human heart manages to keep the terrible peril of suffering at bay.

The author Léon Bloy (+1917) refers to this in his celebrated statement: "There are places in the heart that do not yet exist; suffering has to enter in for them to come to be."[153] Suffering possesses a quickening, an "actualizing" force. It makes us become something more than we are. As St. John Paul II expresses it, "Suffering seems to belong to man's transcendence: it is one of those points in which man is in a certain sense 'destined' to go beyond.... Suffering is...an invitation to manifest the moral greatness of man."[154]

How can this be?

I continue to be struck by an observation of Fr. Julián Carrón: "When I am in endless darkness so much so that I cannot stand myself anymore, it is there that I am forced to go to the bottom of it and recognize an Other."[155] The singular experience of suffering reveals the presence of Someone close to us *in* our suffering. We are not alone in our endless darkness. Divine Love lurks in our agony. And that fact gives us the courage to face any affliction.

On June 2, 1995, Air Force Captain Scott O'Grady was patrolling a no-fly zone over Bosnia. The F-16 he was piloting was hit by a missile fired by a Bosnian Serb mobile rocket launcher. Recalling that moment, O'Grady said, "From the instant that my plane blew up around me, I opened my heart to God's love."[156]

Our essential, innate religiousness comes out through the trauma of suffering. Msgr. Lorenzo Albacete gets to the heart of it:

> Suffering itself is a sign...that you have been violated at the level of your identity. Something should not be. You have a reaction immediately of anger, of wanting to send [suffering] away. Why? If there is no meaning to life, then the question "Why?" doesn't mean anything....
>
> This anger [about suffering] is, I think, a wonderful thing, because it begins and sustains a demand, a quest.... When we face suffering that way...it will bring us to an awareness...of the mystery of human life that [is] otherwise closed.
>
> ...In the end I see that it is a frontier to be crossed to a new level of awareness—about life, about reality, and about what may lie beyond and behind it all.[157]

Viktor E. Frankl, in his eminent book *Man's Search for Meaning*, testifies to this personally. Reflecting on his experiences as a prisoner in a Nazi concentration camp, he writes:

> In some way, suffering ceases to be suffering at the moment it finds a meaning, such as the meaning of a sacrifice....
>
> Man's main concern is not to gain pleasure or to avoid pain but rather to see a meaning in his life. That is why man is even ready to suffer, on the condition, to be sure, that his suffering has a meaning....
>
> The question which beset me [in the concentration camp] was, "Has all this suffering, this dying around us,

a meaning? For, if not, then ultimately there is no meaning to survival; for a life whose meaning depends upon such a happenstance—as whether one escapes or not—ultimately would not be worth living at all.".…

Austrian public-opinion pollsters recently reported that those held in highest esteem by most of the people interviewed are neither the great artists nor the great scientists, neither the great statesmen nor the great sports figures, but those who master a hard lot with their heads held high.[158]

In fact, the ordeal of suffering may be the only thing that puts us in touch with our true self. So says Catholic philosopher Louis Lavelle (+1951):

> Suffering fastens upon our real being firmly and tenaciously; it cuts through all the appearances behind which we hide, until it reaches the depths where the living self dwells.…
>
> In suffering we cling to being more tightly than ever, since every nerve that has not been broken is sensitized to the maximum.…
>
> It is suffering that deepens our consciousness, making it understanding and loving.…
>
> Suffering penetrates to the secret of this most intimate life in the soul.… The real problem is not to find a way to anaesthetize suffering, since that could only be done at the expense…of consciousness itself. The problem is how to transfigure it.…[159]

That "transfiguration" is what Bluegrass superstar Alison Krauss ponders in her rendition of the luminous song/prayer "There Is a Reason":

> Why do we suffer, crossing off the years
> There must be a reason for it all.

...

Hurtin' brings my heart to You, crying with my need,
Depending on Your love to carry me,
The love that shed His blood for all the world to see.
This must be the reason for it all

Hurtin' brings my heart to You, a fortress in the storm.
...
In all the things that cause me pain You give me eyes to see.
...
I've seen hard times and I've been told
There is a reason for it all.[160]

But is there any here-and-now proof that all this is true?

Verification

For the past several years, I have been helping out on Sundays at St. Rose of Lima Church in Newtown, Connecticut, by celebrating Mass. The day of the Sandy Hook school shooting—December 14, 2012—was one that visited excruciating, inexpressible suffering on the families of the twenty children and six teachers who were murdered, on the parish in which eight of the funerals were held, on the whole town, and really on the world.

And yet, almost immediately, good began to appear out of this atrocity. A Presence manifested itself and came close.

For example, a young reporter for the *New Haven Register* named Michael Bellmore was assigned to do a story on St. Rose of Lima Church. He was one of the fallen-away who "hadn't set foot in a Catholic church in ages." He tells the amazing story of getting to church early, seeing a priest, and deciding to go to confession.

> I won't get into the details of my confession, but I will say that it felt good.... It felt good to hear someone say that

everything would be OK, and hearing it from a man of the cloth gave the words a certain clarity. I felt welcome....

I guess you could say I became a relapsed Catholic....

The first thing I did after leaving Mass was to call my mother. I asked her if she wanted to go to church with me on Christmas morning, something we haven't done together in a long time—something I know she's wanted for a long time, too.

It felt like the right thing to do. [161]

Jenny and Matthew Hubbard lost their beautiful little red-headed six-year-old daughter, Catherine Violet, in the rampage. A month after the killing, Jenny somehow found the courage to stand before an assembly of parents of religious education students at St. Rose. She said:

Each time I feel that my tears will not stop, I am pulled back to a place of peace and find comfort that Catherine was called to a job much bigger than I can even fathom. I know that God has a specific purpose for us and while I may not understand right now how I will muster the strength to fulfill His purpose, I must remain centered on His face. He will provide what I need to move forward. He will provide the soft nudges to help me feel confident that I am doing what He intended....

I pray that we find comfort and solace knowing that God loves each one of us and will wrap each one of us in his arms when the days become too much. I pray that the world returns to their faith. [162]

To St. Rose of Lima (+1617) our Lord spoke these words:

Let all [people] know that grace comes after tribulation. Let them know that without the burden of afflictions it is impossible to reach the height of grace. Let them know that the gifts of grace increase as the struggles increase. Let [people] take care not to stray and be deceived. This is the only true stairway to paradise, and without the cross they can find no road to climb to heaven....

If only mortals would learn how great it is to possess divine grace, how beautiful, how noble, how precious.... Without doubt they would devote all their care and concern to winning for themselves pains and afflictions. All [people] throughout the world would seek trouble, infirmities, and torments, instead of good fortune, in order to attain the unfathomable treasure of grace.... No one would complain about his cross or about troubles that may happen to him, if he would come to know the scales on which they are weighed when they are distributed to men.[163]

What the people of Newtown experienced on December 14, 2012, was a share in the cross of Jesus Christ.

CROSS-SHAPED LOVE

As shocking as it sounds, the cross is a sublime gift sent by the Father to his incarnate Son to provide Jesus with a never-to-be-equaled means of demonstrating his love for his Father (and for us!). The cross is love expressed in its highest possible form. Which is why St. John Paul II makes the claim that "if the agony on the Cross had not happened, the truth that God is Love would have been unfounded."[164]

A character in a drama by French playwright Paul Claudel compares the cross to a magnet: "Behold how [the cross] draws everything to itself.... The center and the navel of the world, the element by which all humanity is held together."[165] Cardinal Ratzinger spoke of the cross as "a new center of gravity," because nothing has the power to "ground" us as does Christ's self-sacrificing love.[166]

God the Father offers us too a share in his Son's cross. And Jesus warns us that we are not worthy of God's kingdom unless we daily take up our cross (see Matthew 16:24–26; Mark 8:34–35; Luke 9:23).

Is this some sadistic plan to turn the whole of life into one great nightmare of punishment? Just the opposite! As St. Rose of Lima tells us, the cross is the source of countless joys and delights.

Why exactly is the cross "crucial" to our happiness? One reason is that we constantly wander off the path of what truly satisfies and fulfills us. We get lost and attached and distracted and bogged down by enticing things that turn us away from God and the chance for holiness. We create idols out of possessions, pleasure, power, and prestige. We reduce God to something we can imagine, and control, and manipulate. We make ourselves the measure of all things, and we try to remake God according to our own image.

That is why the cross is a gift, a privilege, a blessing. For us *the cross is God's way of separating us from whatever separates us from God.* The agony of the cross disrupts our life and throws it into turmoil. And thank God it does! Because the cross manages to get our attention. It overturns disenchantment and disillusionment. It forces us to look at our life, to look at what we consider important, and to think through our priorities again. The cross is God's way of repeatedly re-posing a question, the very first words of Jesus in the Gospel of John: "What do you seek?" (John 1:38). Jesus alone is the Answer.

The cross makes it painfully clear what is missing in my life. I am looking for Something More; the happiness and satisfaction my heart craves are still beyond me. The cross won't let me rest until God becomes my all. The cross is God's way of wooing me into true fulfillment. God beckons me to the ultimate joys of life by way of a nonnegotiable death. St. Gregory the Great muses that the return to paradise can be accomplished only by way of mourning.

Another Paul Claudel character, in his play *The Satin Slipper*, states, "The cross will not be satisfied save when it has destroyed in you everything that is not the will of God."[167] This is why Dominican Fr. Simon Tugwell tells us:

> It is the cross and only the cross that provides a constant point of reference in the chaos of our world, because there is all our poverty and helplessness and pain, all our yearning and all our mutual injustice, taken up into the stillness of God's everlasting love and made into the instrument and revelation of his unchanging will.[168]

The Letter to the Hebrews spells out the "logic" of the cross:

> Do not regard lightly the discipline of the Lord,
> nor lose courage when you are punished by him.
> For the Lord disciplines him whom he loves. (Hebrews 12:5–6)

God possesses an uncanny ability to break into our life and disturb things just when we think we've got everything in hand, just when we think we've got it all together. At moments when we become self-satisfied, self-reliant, complacent, content with things just as they are, God sends the cross to shake us up and gain us back. Woe to those who think they have God and his ways all figured out. God is always a surprise.

The author George Bernanos vents about this:

> I know it well: it is not the trial that tears you apart but the resistance you offer to it. I let God snatch away from me anything he wants me to give him. At the first movement of submission, everything becomes serene. Pain thus finds its balance within itself: it is as if it had established itself immovably within the majesty of order.... I am surely not

unaware that God wants all of me, and I always have something I want to keep from him: I make a ridiculous effort to
outwit him. It's as if I were trying to evade his glance, which
he has so firmly settled upon me, forever.[169]

The experience of the cross disciplines us to want at this moment
only what God's love brings to us at this moment. It imposes a
corrective on our judgment, so that we stop making what pleases
us the measure of all things. God loves us *through* the cross of his
Son. In the process he conforms us to himself while at the same time
dis-conforming us from ourselves—a reformation we all need. Pope
Benedict XVI wrote, "The true measure of humanity is essentially
determined in relationship to suffering and to the sufferer."[170]

For at the very least, we often cling to a preconceived idea about
the way life should be. It may be a very proper and good idea, but it
is a conception nonetheless that fails to correspond to the ordained
designs of Divine Providence for us. And eventually all this adds up to
the worst conceivable frustration, and disappointment, and misery.

Eight months after the Sandy Hook School shooting, I had the
privilege of spending a sunny summer afternoon with Jenny Hubbard
and our mutual friend Jane on Jenny's backyard deck. The talk, of
course, turned to her daughter Catherine and how Jenny dealt with
The Question: *Why would God take her?* The certainty and simplicity
of Jenny's response blew me away. She said: *God gave us Catherine
to be with us for six years. Now she is back with God.* This is a true
embrace of the cross of Jesus Christ

Of course, the cross—the whole phenomenon of suffering—remains
forever an immense, unfathomable mystery. Attempts to "explain" it
come off as feeble at best and confirm how only something beyond
reason can get us to the heart of the cross.

Years ago I was teaching a homiletics class at St. Joseph's Seminary
in Dunwoodie, New York. The seminarians' assignment was to

prepare a retreat talk on suffering. One impressive young man (now a wonderful priest), Richard Smith, gave the most amazing presentation.

He based his talk on Caravaggio's famous painting *The Entombment of Christ* (1602–1603). The painting portrays the dead Jesus, along with three men and three women. Two of the men have hold of Christ's body, preparing to lower it into a tomb. The faces of the others convey the gamut of anguish and grief. It is a heartbreaking picture, and as we gaze at this distraught group we wonder how it would ever be possible to make sense of such suffering.

But as we look more closely at the picture, soon-to-be Fr. Smith told us, we see that Caravaggio gives us the answer. The clue comes in the painter's perspective. The entire scene is depicted from below; we are in effect looking up at these seven. It is as if the painter places himself in the open grave in order to give us a glimpse of these woeful goings-on. But more than that, Caravaggio shows us the only adequate way to regard *the phenomenon of suffering itself!* If we want to understand the mystery of suffering symbolized so graphically by the passion of Christ, then we must be willing *to be in the tomb with Jesus!* The *meaning* of suffering comes through our *sharing* in suffering.

St. Paul learned this through painful, personal experience.

> A thorn was given me in the flesh, a messenger of Satan, to harass me, to keep me from being too elated. Three times I begged the Lord about this, that it should leave me; but he said to me, "My grace is sufficient for you, for my power is made perfect in weakness." (2 Corinthians 12:7–9)

Paul recognizes the *value*, the *mercy* of partaking in the passion of Christ, even on a very small level. This conviction moves him to profess:

I will all the more gladly boast of my weaknesses, that the power of Christ may rest upon me. For the sake of Christ, then, I am content with weaknesses, insults, hardships, persecutions, and calamities; for when I am weak, then I am strong. (2 Corinthians 12:9–10)

Reflecting on his own participation in the cross of Jesus, Jacques Fesch shares wisdom indispensable for us:

It is only recently that I have come to understand the meaning of the cross. It is at once prodigious and atrocious: prodigious because it gives us life, and atrocious because if we do not accept to be crucified all life is denied us. This is a great mystery, and blessed are the persecuted.[171]

To *take up* our own cross is to be *caught up* in the act of love that Jesus accomplished on the cross in order to save us from ourselves. As St. John Paul II says in *Dives in Misericordia,*

The cross of Christ...is...a radical revelation of mercy,...of the love that goes against what constitutes the very root of evil in the history of man: against sin and death.

...The cross is like a touch of eternal love upon the most painful wounds of man's earthly existence.[172]

LEARNING HOW TO SUFFER

Cardinal Joseph Ratzinger, in the book *God and the World*, imparts this important counsel:

If we say that suffering is the inner side of love, we then also understand it is so important to *learn how to suffer*— and why, conversely, the avoidance of suffering renders someone unfit to cope with life. He would be left with an existential emptiness, which could then only be combined with bitterness, with rejection, and no longer with any inner acceptance or progress toward maturity.[173]

I would like to propose seven steps for learning how to suffer.

Step 1: Change how you think about suffering. A world without suffering is simply not possible. No one can successfully eradicate suffering from life. Jesus reveals, "In the world you have tribulation" (John 16:33). And about the apostle Paul God promises, "I will show him how much he must suffer for the sake of my name" (Acts 9:16).

As the encyclical *Spe Salvi* teaches:

> We can try to limit suffering, to fight against it, but we cannot eliminate it. It is when we attempt to avoid suffering by withdrawing from anything that might involve hurt, when we try to spare ourselves the effort and pain of pursuing truth, love, and goodness, that we drift into a life of emptiness, in which there may be almost no pain, but the dark sensation of meaninglessness and abandonment is all the greater. It is not by sidestepping or fleeing from suffering that we are healed, but rather by our capacity for accepting it, maturing through it and finding meaning through union with Christ, who suffered with infinite love.[174]

Paul Claudel offers priceless insight to help us change our minds about suffering: "Jesus did not come to explain away suffering, or to remove it. He came to fill it with His presence."[175]

Step 2: Take stock of the suffering you have endured and how it has changed your life for the better. St. Paul is the reigning expert on this:

> Five times I received at the hands of the Jews the forty lashes less one. Three times I have been beaten with rods; once I was stoned. Three times I have been shipwrecked; a night

and a day I have been adrift at sea; on frequent journeys, in danger from rivers, danger from robbers, danger from my own people, danger from Gentiles, danger in the city, danger in the wilderness, danger at sea, danger from false brethren; in toil and hardship, through many a sleepless night, in hunger and thirst, often without food, in cold and exposure. (2 Corinthians 11:24–27)

Does any one of us have a bigger list? Then "who shall separate us from the love of Christ? Shall tribulation, or distress, or persecution, or famine, or nakedness, or peril, or sword?... No, in all these things we are more than conquerors through him who loved us" (Romans 8:35, 37). Suffering makes St. Paul a spiritual giant.

Being "inside" suffering provides a unique and indispensable perspective, as Joseph Ratzinger observes:

> Remarkably enough, the claim that there can no longer be any God, the claim, that is, that God has completely disappeared, is the urgent conclusion drawn by *onlookers* at the terror, the people who view the horrors from the cushioned armchair of their own prosperity and attempt to pay their tribute to it and ward it off from themselves by saying, "If such things can happen, there is no God!"
>
> But among those who are themselves immersed in the fearful reality, the effect is not infrequently just the opposite: it is precisely then that they discover God. In this world of suffering, adoration has continued to rise up.[176]

Step 3: Acknowledge the positive power of suffering. The late Dominican Fr. Servais Pinckaers (+2008)—who was one of the world's foremost moral theologians—captures the positive dimension of suffering vis-à-vis its relationship with happiness:

It is suffering, whether physical, emotional, moral, or spiritual, that brings us in the last analysis to confront the problem of the meaning of our life and to question ourselves about our moral and religious values....

Think of a person who has never known suffering. Is this person real? Or even happy? It seems that solid moral values cannot exist without the experience of suffering, and that suffering is the only gateway to them....

Without suffering, the idea of happiness would be too romantic, too much a thing of the imagination; happiness becomes real only when we are confronted with suffering over the long haul.[177]

Suffering is redemptive: "*In suffering there is concealed* a particular *power that draws a person interiorly close to Christ,* a special grace," St. John Paul II tells us.[178]

Life gives us many wounds, and grace enters *through* the wounds.

Step 4: Get to the heart of your suffering. It's mind boggling that the words below belong to Mother Teresa of Calcutta. Resist the temptation to quit halfway through; the ending makes it all worth it:

Lord, my God, who am I that you should forsake me? The child of your love—and now become as the most hated one— the one you have thrown away as unwanted—unloved. I call, I cling, I want—and there is no One to answer—no One to whom I can cling—no, no One.—Alone. The darkness is so dark—and I am alone.—Unwanted, forsaken.—The loneliness of the heart that wants love is unbearable.... My God—how painful is this unknown pain. It pains without ceasing.... When I try to raise my thoughts to heaven— there is such convicting emptiness that those very thoughts return like sharp knives and hurt my very soul.—Love—the world—it brings nothing.—I am told God loves me—and yet the reality of darkness and coldness and emptiness is so great that nothing touches my soul…. In spite of all—this darkness and emptiness is not as painful as the longing for God.[179]

When all is said and done, even amidst excruciating agony what matters most is "the longing for God." In fact, deprived of the pangs of suffering, could we ever come to a definitive perception of that longing?

Step 5: Love suffering for the spiritual maturity it effects. Doctor of the Church St. Thérèse of Lisieux speaks of her love of suffering: "I thirsted after suffering and I longed to be forgotten."[180] In another place she writes, "Happiness is found only in suffering, and in suffering, moreover, that is unaccompanied by any consolation whatsoever."[181]

We "love" suffering not as masochists but in order to make our *yes* to God and to his mysterious, ever-merciful way of bringing us to full maturity. Cardinal Ratzinger underscores this:

> When we know that the way of love…is the true way by which man becomes human, then we also understand that suffering is the process through which we mature. Anyone who has inwardly accepted suffering becomes more mature and more understanding of others, becomes more human. Anyone who has consistently avoided suffering does not understand other people; he becomes hard and selfish.[182]

Suffering's supreme purpose is to open our soul to God so that we may receive everything from the Father just as Jesus does. What hurts opens our heart. It sunders us from false, or deceiving, or simply inadequate attachments. Suffering makes us feel our nothingness; the poverty of suffering shows us we possess nothing in ourselves by which we could become pleasing to God. Even when we have nothing of our own, we can still say yes to how God acts in our lives.

We love suffering, then, because the essence of suffering is receiving God's love the way he ordains to give that love to us right now. Suffering opens up a space in us by which God can give himself to us that much more.

St. Gregory Nazianzen (+390) sums this up in this pastoral advice: "Worship him who was hung on the cross because of you, even if you are hanging there yourself."[183]

Step 6: Realize the essential role of suffering in your friendship with God. According to a famous story, St. Teresa of Avila was on her way to visit one of her Carmelite monasteries when the horse she was riding reared and threw her off. Disgruntled in the mud, the nun complained to God, "If this is the way you treat your friends, it's no wonder you have so few of them!"

That experience did not keep St. Teresa from exclaiming:

> O my Lord, how you are the true friend; and how powerful!... You never stop loving those who love you!... All things fail; you, Lord of all, never fail!... It seems, Lord, you try with rigor the person who loves you so that in extreme trial she might understand the greatest extreme of your love.... All fails me, my Lord; but if you do not abandon me, I will not fail you. Let all learned men rise up against me, let all created things persecute me, let the devils torment me; do not you fail me, Lord, for I already have experience of the gain that comes from the way you rescue the one who trusts in you alone.[184]

St. Catherine stated with elegant simplicity the ineluctable truth: "Suffering and sorrow increase in proportion to love."[185] *The Imitation of Christ* elaborates on the insight:

Without doubt it is better for you...to be tried in adversities than to have all things as you wish.

...The more spiritual progress a person makes, so much heavier will he frequently find the cross, because as his love increases, the pain of his exile also increases....

With God, nothing that is suffered for His sake, no matter how small, can pass without reward....[186]

Step 7: Rely on suffering in order to grow in charity. St. John Paul II makes the point in *Salvifici Doloris* that love creates good, drawing it out by means of suffering.[187] But if this audacious claim is true, then we should be able to verify it. We should be able to find proof of it in lived experience.

The years between 1978 and 1995 were fraught with particular anxiety for academics, technology experts, and other select individuals in the United States. For that is when a terrorist known as the Unabomber carried out a nationwide bombing spree that killed three people and injured twenty-three others. The twenty-third victim was Yale University professor David Gelernter, who opened a mail bomb sent to his office. Thank God, he survived. And later he wrote these astonishing words:

Although I was hurt permanently and will never get back a normal right hand or right eye—although my chest will always look like a gouged-out construction site—here is the main thing: I recovered. In some ways I am better than before....[188]

If you insert into this weird slot machine of modern life one evil act, a thousand acts of kindness tumble out.[189]

As the mystic Caryll Houselander (+1954) counsels,

Suffering, if we are one with Christ and so offer it in his hands to God, is the most effective of all acts of love.... Christ...came to wed himself to it, to make it inseparable from his redeeming love, one thing with love itself....

It is the most effective gift we have for the good of our fellow men....

The measure in which our own suffering becomes love is not the size of our suffering, but the degree of our oneness with Christ.[190]

We pray for the passion to embrace Christ's passion as did Servant of God Catherine de Hueck Doherty:

For years on end
I wandered through
Deserts hot,
Parched and alone.

For years on end
I climbed cold
Heights and
Measured step
By step
Abysses deep.

For years on end
I walked in
Loneliness too
Deep for words
In search of You.

Then quite suddenly
I came upon You
My All,...my love

Standing naked
Against a whipping post.
Clad only in the crimson
Cloak of blood and pain.

You smiled, and
Bade me stand
Against the other
Side,
Untied, held
Only by the bonds
Of love for you.

I did, and the
Long Roman whips
Cut me apart
And clad me in
The crimson of
My own blood and pain
Yet mingled with
Some drops of Yours.
Because of this
I am still here
At the same whipping post
Of yore.
You are not here.
The drops are
Changed into
Ones of fear and hate
Yet defenseless I remain
Because you still
Mingle your blood with mine
Beloved.[191]

CHAPTER SIX

LOVE AND PRAYER

Looking at the photograph of a sculpture in Chartres Cathedral, God molding Adam, drawn to recollection by the thought that our very loving Father continues to mold us like that right up to the day when our perfection is achieved in heaven. Ah! To stay like that under his gentle hand, our head abandoned on his maternal lap and letting him do as he will with us, always.[192]

—Raïssa Maritain

St. Thérèse of Lisieux tells us that "love is nourished only by sacrifices.... It is prayer, it is sacrifice which give me all my strength; these are the invincible weapons which Jesus has given me."[193] And we need to take them up too!

In speaking of sacrifice, we follow Pope Benedict XVI's lead: "'Sacrifice' in its essence is simply returning to love."[194] Christian sacrifice consists "in our becoming totally receptive and letting ourselves be completely taken over by [God]. Letting God act on us—that is Christian sacrifice."[195]

Some years back I would meet at seven o'clock on Friday mornings with a group of Catholic professionals who come together weekly at that early hour to share the faith and to support each other in being fervent Christian witnesses. We would read and discuss some recommended book. One Friday, as we were talking about prayer, a member of the group—a superior court judge—said simply, "Isn't it something that God *wants* us to pray to him?" That profound insight did more to boost my prayer life than I don't know how many spiritual books I've read.

For the plain fact is that God *desires* communication with us. If for no other reason, we pray to him simply because God wants us to talk to him. He asks us, begs us to. He longs for connection with our heart—communion. The very possibility of prayer is a gift of God's love.

So how are we to pray to stay good friends with God?

ADORATION

To be human is to be a creature designed to adore. Adoration is the fundamental attitude of the human being in respect to God (see *CCC*, 2628). "To adore God is to acknowledge, in respect and absolute submission, the 'nothingness of the creature' who would not exist but for God" (*CCC*, 2097).

One deleterious effect of original sin is that *we* desire to be adored. And unless we do something concretely and continually to counteract that proclivity, the idolatry of egoism takes over. The answer is our adoration of God...especially Eucharistic Adoration! In the words of the *Catechism*, "The worship of the one God sets man free from turning in on himself, from the slavery of sin, and the idolatry of the world" (*CCC*, 2097). And in another place: "Human life finds its unity in the adoration of the one God. The commandment to worship the Lord alone integrates man and saves him from an endless disintegration" (*CCC*, 2114).

Adoration's august ability makes great sense when we take a closer look at the word itself. Pope Benedict XVI explains that "the Latin word for adoration is *ad-oratio*—mouth to mouth contact, a kiss, an embrace, and hence, ultimately love."[196] Adoration is a supreme act of love.

Disfigured by original sin, we constantly try to make *ourselves* the measure of all things. The way out of that trap, Pope Benedict XVI tells us, is adoration, for adoration is "the recognition of God as our true measure."[197] And it is also immensely easy, for all that adoration asks of us is the gift of our nothingness. As Dominican Fr. Antonin Gilbert Sertillanges writes, "The sense of adoration causes the soul to plunge rapturously into the abyss of its nothingness, and that is the very thing it offers to love."[198]

How breathtaking, though, is that sublime form of adoration that is Eucharistic Adoration. Coming before the tabernacle in our nothingness as a beggar; professing our love for One who could have anyone as a friend but who chooses *us*; believing in that election more than in our own inadequacy, failing, and sin; *knowing* that there is someone there in the silence, gazing at us, begging for our heart: This is the true glory of Eucharistic Adoration.

Adoration is like radiation. We go forth from adoration spiritually "radioactive." What's the opposite of "contaminate?" Whatever it is, as the result of our contact with the Presence alive in the Blessed Sacrament, that's what we do to everyone we encounter. For we *become* that presence in a different way. We radiate to others the invisible power that has taken hold of us and transfigured our deepest self through union with the real presence.

Our Unceasing Act of Love

One sure way of cultivating a life of adoration is by being committed to making *an unceasing act of love*. Our mandate for this comes directly from St. Paul: "Rejoice always, pray constantly, give thanks in all circumstances; for this is the will of God in Christ Jesus for you" (1 Thessalonians 5:16–18).

The unceasing act of love is as old as Our Lady's *fiat* to the archangel Gabriel: *Let it be to me according to your word* (Luke 1:38—which is why the Church prays perpetually the *Angelus*!). The unceasing act of love is our concrete, actual gesture of loving God—our handing over of our heart in an intentional gift of self to God moment by moment, so that it becomes our very *modus vivendi*. We want the gift of self to God to be habitual, total—to become second nature.

The fourteenth-century Rhineland Dominican mystic Blessed Henry Suso endorses this:

> A seasoned friend of God should always have some good... saying in the mouth of his soul to chew on that will inflame his heart for God, because therein lies the most sublime thing we can attain on earth—that we often reflect on our divine Beloved, that we often send out our hearts to him, often speak of him, take in his words of love.... Our eye should look upon him with love. Our ear should open to his bidding. Our heart, mind, and spirit should lovingly embrace him. If we make him angry, we should beg his pardon. If he tries us, we should endure him. When he hides, we should seek our dear Love and never give up until we find him again and again. When we find him, we should hold him tenderly and reverently.... Realize that this is the best habit you can have, for constant prayer is the crown of all activity. Everything else should be directed to it as to its goal. What other activity is there in heaven but gazing at and loving the object of all love, loving it and praising it? Therefore, the more dearly we press the divine object of our love into our hearts, and the more often we look upon him and intimately embrace him with the arms of our hearts, the more lovingly shall we be embraced by him here and in our eternal happiness.[199]

One celebrated unceasing act of love is the "Jesus Prayer," made famous by the nineteenth-century spiritual classic *The Way of the Pilgrim*. As the pilgrim of the tale journeys across Russia on foot, he matches his inhaling and exhaling with the invocations of the prayer: *Lord, Jesus Christ, Son of the living God, have mercy on me, a sinner*. He repeats the prayer incessantly until it becomes one with his breath, his very self.

Why the holy name of Jesus? The fourteenth-century English mystic Richard Rolle answers with eloquence:

> If you will be well with God, and have grace to rule your life,
> and come to the joy of love:
> this name Jesus, fasten it so fast in your heart
> that it come never out of your thought.
> And when you speak to him, and through custom say, "Jesus,"
> it shall be in your ear, joy;
> in your mouth, honey;
> and in your heart, melody:
> for [people] shall think joy to hear that name be named,
> sweetness to speak it, mirth, and song to think it.
>
> If you think the name "Jesus" continually, and hold it firmly,
> it purges your sin, and kindles your heart;
> it clarifies your soul, it removes anger and does away slowness.
> It wounds in love and fulfills charity.
>
> It chases the devil, and puts out dread.
> It opens heaven, and makes a contemplative man.
> Have Jesus in mind, for that puts all vices and phantoms out from the lover.[200]

Why "unceasing" prayer? Because if we are not *actually* loving God, we are *actually* loving something else in his place. ("No one can serve two masters," Matthew 6:24.) For we are made for love. In a talk I once heard, my friend Chris Bacich said, "Any moment in which we are not crying out to the Infinite is in some way a moment of despair."

The minute we give up our unceasing act of love is the moment our life begins to fall apart. When we fall off offering our act of love, we fall back into ourselves—into our own inadequate thoughts, our own imperfect understanding of things, our compromises and false idols. When we give up our act of love, then we try to rely on our own faulty strength. That's when concupiscence starts to assert itself and temptations take over. That's when our fears and anxieties begin to dominate us. That's when we presume to trust our own reasons, our preconceptions, and our feelings instead of confiding in the Truth who is Jesus. We in effect paralyze God in our regard through our indifference and unresponsiveness to him. God can't give himself to us unless we want him.

Conversely, our unceasing act of love gives God the freedom *to be* God in our lives. When our love for God is actual moment by moment, we dispose ourselves to receive God's love. And God will always respect our freedom; he will never force himself on us.

The act of love takes us out of ourselves and unites us to our Beloved, to Jesus. It satisfies our otherwise insatiable desire to be adored. This is why the heart of Christmas is *O, come let us adore him!* As the *Catechism* teaches: "No one, whether shepherd or wise man, can approach God here below except by kneeling before the manger at Bethlehem and adoring him hidden in the weakness of a new-born child" (CCC, 563).

Making an act of love is the easiest thing in the world! And we can do so even when we do not "feel" that we love God. As St. Thérèse teaches us: "Do not be afraid to tell Jesus that you love him—even if you don't feel that you love him. That is the way to force him to aid you."[201] And St. Francis de Sales gives this wise counsel: "Perform fervent external actions, even though you may perform them without relish, such as embracing the crucifix.... Sometimes you may arouse your heart by some position or action of exterior devotion."[202]

Abbé Berlioux (+1885), in his *Month of the Sacred Heart*, gives us this direction:

> Jesus has promised that he will cure and save all those who invoke with confidence his Sacred Heart, yes, even lukewarm souls; he will cast down upon you a spark of love, and you will be restored to fervor and life. Say often to your merciful Savior: O Jesus! *he whom you love is sick, come and heal him*, and Jesus will give back to you the strength and fervor of your early years; take courage, then, and throw yourself into this divine heart.[203]

Our invocation can take the simplest of forms, like the one I use at every stray moment of the day: *Jesus and Mary, I love you! Save souls!*

LECTIO DIVINA

To love God is to listen devotedly to his Word. That means prayerfully reading Sacred Scripture as a regular part of our spiritual life—even if it is only a page or two a day. There we hear the voice of God speaking to us personally. There we see the face of God.

The Bible is more than a book—it is a Presence, a Person. The love letter of the Bible is written to move us at the level of our heart, not just our head.

In reflecting on *lectio divina* (sacred reading), the esteemed theologian Fr. Louis Bouyer (+2004), whose classic must-read *Introduction to the Spiritual Life* is back in print, stresses that, in every word of God, what matters most is God's opening his own heart to us. St. Thérèse of Lisieux declares: "No sooner do I glance at the Gospel, but immediately I breathe in the fragrance of the life of Jesus and I know where to run."[204]

As you take up Sacred Scripture to pray it, so as to dispose yourself to all the graces it offers, why not begin with a prayer like this:

> Holy Spirit of Truth,
> the Word of God creates in me
> the capacity to receive the action
> by which you apply the saving events of Jesus Christ
> to my life right now.
> Make me open to that action.
> Make me attentive and sensitive
> to every divine whisper of love in this biblical text.
> Inspire my mind and illumine my heart,
> that I may pierce the pearl of this Holy Scripture
> and penetrate the inner dimension of God's glorious Word,
> so that the events of the Redemption
> experienced in person by Christ's disciples
> when he walked this earth
> —events that never end!—
> may reach me with now by Word.

The ninth-century Benedictine monk Ardo Smaragdus captures why every lover of God must engage in *lectio divina*:

> [*Lectio divina*] sharpens the perception, enriches understanding, rouses from sloth, banishes idleness, orders life, corrects bad habits, produces salutary weeping and draws tears from contrite hearts...curbs idle speech and vanity, awakens longing for Christ and the heavenly homeland.[205]

Or in the words of Pope Benedict XVI in *Verbum Domini*, "In the Word of God...Jesus says today, here and now, to each person: 'I am yours, I give myself to you;' so that we can receive and respond, saying in return: 'I am yours.'"[206]

MARIAN DEVOTION

We *have* to pray to the Blessed Virgin Mary, for she is the only human person, with her singular Immaculate Heart, who is capable of loving Jesus Christ the way he deserves to be loved. We *must* cultivate a deep, abiding devotion to Mary, whom the crucified Jesus has given to us to be our mother.

There are about a million reasons for this. But I do not think I have ever come across a more compelling explanation than that of Myles Connolly (+1964) in his powerful, mystical book *Mr. Blue*:

> My good dear Mother:... You are more real to me than the people around me.... Mother, you are so real that if you withdrew your support I think I would actually fall down on the floor here like a man in a faint.... Only for you, I would have long been lost. For you it is who took me and led me out of strange ways and darknesses years ago. You it is who takes me by the hand now day by day. Only you would not grow tired of the like of me—of anyone so sinful, ungrateful, selfish.... I would not dare to lift my head were it not for you.... The thought of my sins smites me down so that if there were not you I think I would fall into despair. And when I try to reason why you should continue to protect me, I end in confusion. I can only throw myself on your love. I can only kneel and cry out: "I don't deserve anything. Not even the greeting of a stranger. But, Mother, without you what am I going to do?" This is mad, isn't it? This is unreasonable. But I am helpless in my weakness. I, cowardly, feebly, selfishly, give the weight of my sins to you.... Never was there a worse sinner, and never was God kinder to one. Mother, it's true. You know how true it is. You are the only explanation of God's kindness to me.[207]

PRAY FOR A HOLY LIFE

On a retreat some years ago, I went to confession to a wise old priest who gave me some of the most simple but also most profound counsel I can remember. He told me to spend ten minutes of prayer every day asking God to show me how much he loves me. It has made all the difference.

St. Thomas Aquinas's certainty about God's love shines through in his beautiful prayer for leading a holy life:

> Grant to me, O my God, that I may turn my heart to you always, and grieve for my failings with a firm purpose of amendment. Make me, O Lord, obedient without opposition; poor without repining; chaste without blemish; patient without murmur; humble without pretense; merry without riotousness; serious without heaviness; cheerful without frivolity; God-fearing without abjectness; truthful without duplicity; doing good without presumption; correcting my neighbor without pride; edifying him by word and example without hypocrisy.
>
> Grant to me, O Lord God, a vigilant heart that no subtle speculation may ever lead me from you; a nobleness that no unworthy affection may draw from you; a rectitude that no evil purpose may turn from you. Grant me a steadfastness which no tribulation may shatter; a freedom that no violent affection may overthrow. Give me, O Lord my God, a mind to know you, diligence to seek you, wisdom to find you. Give me a way of life pleasing to you, perseverance to trust and await you, and finally faith to embrace you.[208]

CHAPTER SEVEN

LOVING OUR NEIGHBOR

If we have seen a little child caress his mother's cheek with a small, tender hand, we have seen how we should touch a sinner who might have faith, or a leper who might thank God. We must love them.[209]

—SERVANT OF GOD MOTHER MARY ALPHONSA
(ROSE HAWTHORNE)

You shall love the Lord your God with all your heart, and with all your soul, and with all your mind.... You shall love your neighbor as yourself. (Matthew 22:37, 39)

A new commandment I give to you, that you love one another; even as I have loved you, that you also love one another. (John 13:34)

Here's the thing: Left to myself and to my own devices, I don't *want* to love my neighbor. In fact I *can't*. I don't have what it takes.

But as much as that may be so, here is the greater truth: *I myself want to be loved that way!* I want to be loved when I don't deserve it. I want to be loved gratuitously (because of the goodness of another). I want to be loved without limit. I want to be loved by others the way that the Son of God himself has loved and does love all people.

As inconvenient as it may seem, there is no escaping the Golden Rule: "Whatever you wish that men would do to you, do so to them" (Matthew 7:12). St. John lays bare the logic: "If any one says, 'I love God,' and hates his brother, he is a liar; for he who does not love his brother whom he has seen, cannot love God whom he has not seen" (1 John 4:20).

The author Charles Péguy (+1914) puts his finger on the deception to which we so easily cede: "Because they love no one, they delude themselves into thinking they love God."[210] But all the great spiritual masters, like St. John of the Cross and St. Thérèse of Lisieux, keep reminding us without pause: "At the evening of our life we will be judged on love."[211]

So I *will* love my neighbor, because I recognize that what I need so desperately for myself is something I must give to others. The new commandment is not just a "commandment"; it is a share in God's own being—it is divine, efficacious power from heaven transforming my weakness and blessing me with a supernatural endowment that exceeds all my limitations. Christ commands me to do only what he himself makes possible for me to do.

The Beatitudes (see Matthew 5:3–12) provide a perfect pattern for concretely loving our neighbor. For in the Beatitudes we experience first God's love for *us: how* God loves us and *why.* And the experience of that titanic love immediately moves us to share it. The more we give God's love away as the gift that it is, the more it becomes our own—the more it takes hold of us.

In the ecstasy of that superabundant divine love, we feel moved to offer it to others. God's love burns in us like a fire, a fire we never want to put out. We *give out* the very love we have received in order to keep the blaze aflame.

We become like a new father who, in his euphoria over the birth of his firstborn child, can't help but pass out cigars as he announces to the world the blessed event. To live the gift of his newborn baby, he has to give gifts to others. Only that actual sharing of himself honors the reality of the event, makes his joy grow, and keeps his elation "true."

The Beatitudes reveal to us how the blessed are called to bless others with the blessedness of charity they have received from God.

"Blessed are the poor in spirit, for theirs is the kingdom of heaven" (Matthew 5:3).

God's love came to us when we were destitute. We did nothing to deserve it or earn it. If our indigence teaches us anything, it is that God prefers us precisely *because* we are poor. Our poverty convinces us that God is Love. The fact of our being loved by God is explainable only by the generosity of *his* goodness. In our nothingness we have no *a priori* claim on God's love.

Poverty is rooted in the fundamental awareness that to be myself, I need something more than myself. I must reach out to One greater than myself and beg from him what I lack. We call this movement *morality*, and it is what makes the poor blessed.

The love of God came to us when we were beggars. Our inability to "pay back" God for his love is proof of how much it is a sublime, gratuitous gift.

Similarly, we don't love others with our own love but with the love of God, which God himself gives us. As Pope Benedict XVI says in his encyclical on love, *Deus Caritas Est*, "Anyone who wishes to give love must also receive love as a gift."[212] With that gift comes the blessed ability to love others as God himself loves them.

When Jesus commands us to love one another as he has loved us, he means literally that we are to love one another *with his love*. We know from personal experience just how inadequate and deficient our own love is. That is why the Lord gives us his own love with which to love others. As St. Thérèse of Lisieux expresses it in her autobiography:

> It is...a question of loving one's neighbor as *he, Jesus, has loved him*, and will love him to the consummation of the ages....
>
> Never would I be able to love my Sisters [the other nuns in the Carmel] as you love them unless *you*, O my Jesus, *loved*

them in me. It is because you wanted to give me this grace that you made your *new* commandment. Oh! how I love this new commandment since it gives me the assurance that your will is *to love in me* all those you command me to love![213]

God's extravagance toward us in our poverty calls for like lavishness in our loving others. I treasure a line from the thirteenth-century Dominican friar William Peraldus: "Everything is for giving away."[214] Everything. Because God has loved me, and I want to be true to his love, I give you whatever I have: my belongings, my money, my time, my lane on the highway, my attention, my need to be right in a discussion, my help, dibs on the last pork chop, forgiveness, sympathy, recognition, thanks, and my yen to be first, best, esteemed.

Because God has loved me in my poverty—and because that love has made all the difference—I will turn the other cheek, I will let you have my coat and my cloak as well, I will go the extra mile, I will give to you when you beg from me (see Matthew 5:39–42). In my acceptance of that voluntary poverty, you will be struck, you will wonder why, *you will feel loved!* You will realize that I do these things not because I am a "philanthropist" or "do-gooder" or "humanitarian" but because I am loved by a Love greater than anything I have given up. And what I want more than anything else is for you to embrace that Love too. (And then I get to experience that Love even more *through you!*)

The famous poor widow who puts her life savings of two copper coins into the temple treasury (Mark 12:41–44): Notice that she is not identified as "an old woman" or "a female senior citizen" or "an elderly lady of the congregation." Rather she is identified as a "poor widow." Why? Because her life is defined by *love*.

The widow has nothing, but everything she has is for giving away. The love she would have gladly spent on her husband and children, she spends in helping the poor as a concrete expression of how God has loved her and of how she loves God.

"Blessed are those who mourn, for they shall be comforted" (Matthew 5:4).

Sometimes our mourning flows from taking things for granted. At base, our mourning is the expression of deep remorse at our presumption, our lack of wonder, our arrogance toward things, our cynicism. The familiar scene of the regretful bereaved survivor standing at a coffin begging forgiveness from the deceased recurs throughout literature.

The Cloud of Unknowing counsels:

> He alone feels authentic sorrow who realizes not only *what he is* but *that he is*. Anyone who has not felt this should really weep, for he has never experienced real sorrow. This sorrow purifies a man of sin and sin's punishment. Even more, it prepares his heart to receive that joy through which he will finally transcend the knowing and feeling of his being.[215]

We mourn when a love that means everything to us is taken away. We are blessed in our mourning, as there we come to realize how much we need God's love. Our mourning is a cry of holy dependence. Mourning makes us mindful of the love we are made for. It predisposes us to receive that love.

When we live from the memory of our mourning—"memory" being the ability to enter into the depth of an event and see what could not be seen on a merely superficial level[216]—we want to love others in a way that preserves them from such sorrow.

Our best love for others will always flow from our remembrance of our own loss, woundedness, hardship, powerlessness, anguish, failure, and sorrow. As St. Paul testifies, "The Father of mercies and God of all comfort...comforts us in all our affliction, so that we may be able to comfort those who are in any affliction, with the comfort with which we ourselves are comforted by God" (2 Corinthians 1:3–4).

Some of the most shocking words Jesus ever speaks are to a widow engulfed in grief: "Do not weep" (Luke 7:13). Isn't this the height of insensitivity? The woman's husband has died; now she has lost her only child; she has no means of support—most likely she will soon be out on the street. If there is any time for weeping, it is now!

Unless all the loss she mourns is going to be returned to her in a way she never could have imagined. And that is exactly what Jesus does for her. "'Young man, I say to you, arise.'... And he gave him to his mother" (Luke 7:14, 15).

Feelings of grief do not impede our ability to love. In fact, they intensify and even aggravate our need for love. Our experience of mourning shows us that love is more than a feeling; rather it is a choice of how we look at reality. That's what Jesus summons from the widow of Nain: *Either you can wallow in your weeping, or you can let your mourning lead you to a newness of life beyond your dreams.*

What happened, I wonder, in the weeks and months following the wondrous raising of the widow's son? Doesn't it make sense that the widow of Nain went on to become a champion of charity, especially in consoling the most downtrodden, trial ridden, and despairing? Why? Because every speck of love she gave to others came directly from the grave of her own former pain.

There is no way the widow could have kept to herself the astounding miracle of love she experienced at the hands of Jesus Christ, all because she was mourning. The love that was given back into her arms she went on to give away to others. Maybe she even passed out to everyone wristbands that read, *Do not weep!*

Deus Caritas Est states:

Love is not merely a sentiment.... God does not demand of us a feeling which we ourselves are incapable of producing. He loves us, he makes us see and experience his love, and since he has "loved us first," love can also blossom as a response within us.[217]

Thank God for blessed mourning, which makes us realize that Love has loved us first and that moves love to blossom within us.

In George Bernanos's novel *Diary of a Country Priest*, the young pastor of the remote French village visits Madame la Comtesse to offer her some spiritual solace. The woman is bitter and antagonistic, torn apart by unyielding grief over the loss of her only son when he was but a little boy. Her plight is dire: She is headed for a hell of alienation and atheism. There seems to be no way out, until the priest says something that proceeds from his own personal experience of profound misery:

The lowest of human beings, even though he no longer thinks he can love, still has in him the power of loving....

God is love itself.... If you want to love, don't place yourself beyond love's reach.[218]

These words resurrect her.

"Blessed are the meek, for they shall inherit the earth" (Matthew 5:5).

What is meekness? The meek are those who know how to manage and order anger, those who do not live by their passions. One of the greatest acts of charity we can offer our neighbor is simply not to return anger when another exhibits anger toward us.

But how can we do this? Meekness remains something totally foreign to us in our fallen state. Without the aid of grace, we would completely cave in to the slavery of our passions.

The meek are meek because they have allowed something greater than anger to dominate their lives. Fr. Walter Hilton tells us what that is. In *The Scale of Perfection* he writes:

> When love acts in the soul it does so wisely and gently, for it has great power to kill anger and envy, and all the passions of wrath and melancholy, and it brings into the soul the virtues of patience, gentleness, peaceableness, and friendliness to one's neighbor.
>
> People guided only by their own reason find it very hard to be patient, peaceful, sweet-tempered, and charitable to their neighbors when they treat them badly and wrong them. But true lovers of Jesus have no great difficulty in enduring all this, because love fights for them and kills such movements of wrath and melancholy with amazing ease.
>
> Through the spiritual sight of Jesus it makes the souls of such people so much at ease and so peaceful, so ready to endure and so conformed to God, that if they are despised and disregarded by others, or suffer injustice or injury, shame or ill-treatment, they pay no attention.
>
> They are not greatly disturbed by these things and will not allow themselves to be, for then they would lose the comfort they feel in their souls, and that they are unwilling to do. They can more easily forget all the wrong that is done them than others can forgive it even when asked for forgiveness. They would rather forget than forgive, for that seems easier to them.[219]

Without question, the most shocking thing about the parable of the prodigal son is the response of the father to *both* sons' homecomings. Not only is the father utterly lacking in any anger or even irritation, but he even goes to the extreme of making a fool of himself by running in public in order to accelerate the reconciliation with his wayward, returning younger son. In place of fury, rage, and retribution, the father showers his son with gifts of a robe, a ring, and sandals. The only one who "gets it" is the fatted calf, and that's so that they all can feast.

The older son, upon learning all this, is the total opposite of meek: He is consumed with ire, indignation, resentment. Openly upset and annoyed, he vents his temper on his father. But here again the consummate meekness of the man wins the day. And it moves us to wonder: *What could ever transfigure someone so completely that hostility and vengeance don't stand a chance?*

Only one answer makes sense: The father *himself* must have been loved that way before. It has made him meek. And in his meekness he remains a world-class bearer of patience and compassion.

One day a friend of Msgr. Luigi Giussani was talking with the priest. He shared a doubt: He was beginning to wonder if he *really* loved his family. Msgr. Giussani asked him if he loved his children. When the man replied that he did, Msgr. Giussani told him to give an example of this love. The man spoke about coming home late from work, peering into the bedroom where his little children were sleeping, being overcome by an unfathomable tenderness for them, hugging them. To this Msgr. Giussani replied:

> The real way to love is that right in those moments when this tenderness is intense, real, and overwhelming, humanly overwhelming, you should step back and look at them and say, "What will become of them?" because loving means understanding that they have a destiny, that they don't belong to you, they are yours and they're not yours, they have a destiny and it is precisely by looking at the dramatic nature which destiny imposes on relationships and things, on the future and the present, that you will respect them,

you will love them, you will be ready to do anything for them, you won't give in to the blackmail of whether they obey you or not.[220]

In other words, the real way to love is to love not from our passions but from the meekness that is itself a confirmation of how much divine Love has claimed us.

"Blessed are those who hunger and thirst for righteousness, for they shall be satisfied" (Matthew 5:6).

"Righteousness" means walking with Jesus so that we come to share personally the very righteousness of our Christ. We didn't always walk this way, but deep down it is what we always truly craved. Then one day Jesus came to us—even if not as dramatically as he did to St. Paul on the road to Damascus—and he claimed us. He beckoned us to share his own righteousness. It has become our daily bread. To live that righteousness is to love others through it, and with it, and in it.

We best experience our hunger and thirst for righteousness when we desire good for others. In the words of the Roman philosopher Seneca: "If you want to live for yourself, you must live for another."[221]

Servant of God Dorothy Day once wrote:

> I really only love God as much as I love the person I love the least.[222]

> We cannot love God unless we love each other, and to love we must know each other. We know him in the breaking of bread, and we know each other in the breaking of bread, and we are not alone anymore.[223]

But again, who in the world can do this? Only someone who has been given a new nature, a righteousness that changes and perfects to the core, so as to make one "perfect, as your heavenly Father is perfect"

(Matthew 5:48). The perfection of God the Father consists in his mercifully loving others who deserve love not at all. This is divine righteousness.

Is this possible for me? Pope Benedict XVI answers *yes!* How? Through the hunger for righteousness that Christ's love ignites in me:

> I love even the person whom I do not like or even know. This can only take place on the basis of an intimate encounter with God, an encounter which has become a communion of will, even affecting my feelings. Then I learn to look on this other person not simply with my eyes and my feelings, but from the perspective of Jesus Christ. His friend is my friend. Going beyond exterior appearances, I perceive in others an interior desire for a sign of love, of concern. This I can offer them.... I can give them the look of love which they crave....[224]

Aptly, righteousness is described in terms of hunger. If we ignore our hunger we starve. The confirmation that we are feeding that hunger, St. Gregory the Great tells us, is that we are accomplishing works of love for our neighbor. He writes, "The proof of love is one's actions. Love for God is never lazy: if it is present it accomplishes great things; if it refuses to work, it will not love."[225] To love God it is necessary to use our words, our minds, and our lives.

"Blessed are the merciful, for they shall obtain mercy" (Matthew 5:7).

We have already discussed love and mercy. We can reemphasize here that loving our neighbor means loving him or her through the forgiveness we have ourselves received.

The model for this is Christ's parable of the sheep and the goats (Matthew 25:31–46). The parable suggests that we have a *choice* whether to be self-absorbed goats or self-giving sheep. The goats are as oblivious to their dereliction toward the needy as the sheep are to the fact that, in loving the disadvantaged, they in fact are serving Jesus himself.

What transformed the sheep from their "goatness"? Well, maybe they were once *the lost sheep* (see Matthew 18:10–14). And maybe a super-merciful Good Shepherd came one perilous day and found them when they were hanging from a cliff, snatched them to safety, and carried them home. That experience of being rescued, that miracle of mercy, becomes the memory from which they perpetually live. It makes them likewise loving and merciful *by second nature,* for the rest of their lives.

Every time the sheep show a similar act of mercy to the starving, the stranger, the naked, or the imprisoned, they relive that saving event of being found. And the original event of mercy happens all over again. In turn it makes them want to be lavish in showing mercy to others. That generosity keeps them ever sensitive to the Love who gave them new life.

The sheep regard every person in need as someone wanted by God like themselves, someone whom the Good Shepherd reaches out to *precisely because* that person is lost and on the brink of the abyss. That is how mercy changes us.

As Pope Benedict XVI understands it,

> Love of neighbor is a path that leads to the encounter with God....
>
> Only my readiness to encounter my neighbor and to show him love makes me sensitive to God as well. Only if I serve my neighbor can my eyes be opened to what God does for me and how much he loves me.[226]

"Blessed are the pure in heart, for they shall see God" (Matthew 5:8).

The pure in heart are blessed because they permit themselves to be loved the way that God ordains to love us: in total purity of heart. Purity of heart means willing one thing: the good. God loves us with the love called *agape*: a self-giving love that exalts the good of the other gratuitously without counting the cost.

Begotten in the purity of God's love, we become pure. The philosopher Louis Lavelle describes what this means:

> Purity penetrates into the innermost recesses of the soul, dissolving the scum of egoism, the accumulations of wrong desires, the mixture of fear, suspicion, and baseness which prejudices had formed in us in spite of ourselves....
>
> The opposite of purity is anxiety, which unfailingly creates a division in the soul; but purity abolishes all strife between the soul and herself.... Purity is the quality of the child who freely shows us his inner self, before the process of repression and distortion has set in....
>
> The perfection of purity...proves its strength and efficacy by passing through all uncleanness in the world...leaving in its midst its own radiance.[227]

The gift of purity of heart came to Zacchaeus while perched high in his sycamore tree (see Luke 19:1–10). "Blessed are the pure of heart, for they shall see God." And what does the Gospel indicate about Zacchaeus? "He ran on ahead and climbed up into a sycamore tree to see [Jesus]."

But it is *Jesus* who does the real seeing: "And when Jesus came to the place, he looked up and said to him, 'Zacchaeus, make haste and come down; for I must stay at your house today.'" As Zacchaeus scurries down the trunk, he sheds his crippling egoism, his evil desires, his baseness, and his anxiety. Purity penetrates into the recesses of his soul; he freely shows his radiant inner self.

The proof of it is his desire to share it. Like an irrepressible little child, he declares: "Behold, Lord, the half of my goods I give to the poor."

Since God generates such purity in us from the bounty of his love, we too are eager to engender in others that purity. Which means loving others *without reducing them*—without manipulating, or using, or possessing them. When we love others in purity of heart, we desire to preserve and protect all that is good and beautiful and godly in them. God's love for us is the very thing that has enabled us to *become ourselves* fully. That is the very gift we want to offer others by loving them in purity of heart.

We best understand what it means to love others in purity of heart when we think about how *we ourselves* want to be loved by others. We long to be loved without the imposition of conditions, loved without measure, loved without the lover's counting the cost. We desire to be loved for ourselves, not for what others can get from us.

St. John XXIII said that purity of heart "must be the breath of the love of God, and the indispensable condition for disinterested service to our neighbor."[228]

We love other people for one unalterable reason: because every human person *is* a relationship with God. We do not love others because of what they can do for us, or because we are attracted to them, or because we can benefit from their acquaintance. We love them gratuitously, that is, we love them because of *who they are.*

To be human is to be someone wanted by God. The pure of heart see this.

"Blessed are the peacemakers, for they shall be called sons of God" (Matthew 5:9).

When Jesus Christ rises from the dead, he comes and stands among his disciples, and he says to them, "Peace be with you" (John 20:19,

21). This is not merely some cordial greeting; it is the bestowal of a divine, life-altering gift—the first fruit of the Resurrection.

Peace is the grace that blesses us with the facility to enter into a new and lasting friendship with others, especially those from whom we were formerly estranged. Peace is the restoration of what is required in order to live a relationship of serenity and amity with others. Peace removes whatever makes us feel like strangers, eliminates obstructions, rectifies alienation, and clears away discord. Peace rehabilitates our capability to live in harmony and deep communion with another.

Why are these words of peace the first to come from the lips of the risen Christ? St. Thomas Aquinas identifies the precise heart of charity: "We wish that our neighbor may be in God."[229] By pronouncing peace, Jesus reveals this very wish for those who deserted and denied him. We, in effect, *become* this peace.

To love our neighbor is to proffer to him or her the same heavenly gift of peace that we have received from our resurrected Savior. This is the significance of the Sign of Peace at Mass.

How exactly do we "make peace"? By engaging in intentional acts of charity—acts that reinsert in the world what is missing or broken so that harmony and communion may flourish again. Msgr. Giussani makes clear this integral link between the restorative capacity of peace and our ultimate motive for engaging in charitable work:

> 1. When there is something beautiful within us, we desire to communicate it to others. When we see others who are worse off than we are, we desire to help them with something of ours. This need is so original, so natural, that it is within us before we are conscious of it…. We do charitable work to satisfy this need.
>
> 2. We become ourselves to the extent that we live this need and this requirement. Communicating to others gives us the experience of completing ourselves. This is so true that, if we

are not able to give, we experience ourselves as incomplete beings.

To be interested in others, to communicate to others, enables us to fulfill the supreme and, indeed, the only task in life: to become ourselves, to complete ourselves. We do charitable work so that we may learn to fulfill the task of becoming ourselves.

3. But it is Christ who has enabled us to understand the ultimate reason for this, revealing the ultimate law of being and of life: charity. The supreme law of our being is to share in the being of others, to live in communion.... We do charitable work in order to live like Christ.[230]

"Blessed are those who are persecuted for righteousness' sake, for theirs is the kingdom of heaven" (Matthew 5:10).

Jesus announces to his apostles what will come to be forever the world's preeminent persecution: his passion. But Peter reacts badly: "God forbid, Lord! This shall never happen to you" (Matthew 16:22). Jesus responds, "Get behind me, Satan! You are a hindrance to me; for you are not on the side of God" (Matthew 16:23).

Peter does not yet comprehend the persecution "for righteousness' sake" that is the cross. But he will come to understand it in his very flesh. And it is Peter's personal participation in "persecution for righteousness' sake" that will make his post-Easter life of charity so compelling and effective.

In loving our neighbor, we must remain vigilant to any impulse that threatens to turn us against God and the mysterious workings of his divine will. Perhaps we would never openly defy Jesus as Peter does in his reckless outburst, but there exist other subtle, seductive, insidious attitudes that can land us on the side of Satan, harming our neighbor in the process. Chief among them is *the spirit of derision*.

Dominican Fr. Reginald Garrigou-Lagrange (+1964) describes it:

> Among the causes of tepidity in [lax] souls, the tendency to derision should be particularly noted. St. Thomas speaks of the derider when he discusses the vices opposed to justice: insult, detraction, murmuring against the reputation of our neighbor. He points out that to deride or to ridicule someone is to show that we do not esteem him; and derision, says the saint, may become a mortal sin if it affects persons or things that deserve high esteem....
>
> The derider is himself a [lax] soul, holding others back and becoming, often without being aware of it, the instrument of the spirit of evil. His cast of soul, which is the direct opposite of evangelical simplicity, is the one most opposed to supernatural contemplation. The derider, who wishes "to play the rogue," ridicules the just man who tends truly to perfection; he emphasizes the latter's defects and depreciates his good qualities. Why is this? Because he feels that he himself has little virtue, and he is unwilling to admit his inferiority. Then, out of spite, he lessens the real and fundamental value of his neighbor and the necessity of virtue itself. He may greatly harm weak souls which he intimidates, and, while working his own ruin, he may labor at their perdition.[231]

It is the exceptional goodness of the Lord that offends the opponents of Jesus Christ, infecting them with the demonic plot to kill him. That same disease threatens to taint us unless we accept the cross as something to embrace, not repel. Only the love that pours from the cross can kill the sloth and envy (two of the seven deadly sins) that would otherwise kill us. Persecution is a purification—a great, earth-shattering grace!

We will not permit the fear of persecution to turn us into a derider. The righteousness that keeps begging for our hearts with the words *Do you love me?* returns us to our true self, exchanging any lingering trace of laxity for the fever of charity burning in our Beloved's gaze.

"Blessed are you when men revile you and persecute you and utter all kinds of evil against you falsely on my account. Rejoice and be glad, for your reward is great in heaven" (Matthew 5:11–12).

How is being reviled and persecuted a sign that God loves us? The apostles clearly understood maltreatment as such, for the Acts of the Apostles recounts that "they left the presence of the council, rejoicing that they were counted worthy to suffer dishonor for the name" (Acts 5:41).

Of course, Jesus himself revealed this the night before he died: "I chose you out of the world, therefore the world hates you" (John 15:19). Early on the Lord had warned, "Woe to you, when all men speak well of you" (Luke 6:26).

Love blesses us with a "vital participation" (see CCC, 2842) in the persecution that is Christ's passion. It generates in us a new judgment on reality that equips us to face the crisis we will inevitably confront with the only force powerful enough to counter it: divine charity. And since "the opposite of love is not hate, it's indifference," [232] our charity toward our persecutors must be proactive.

St. John Chrysostom (+407) identifies nine degrees of our love of enemies:

1. Not to start giving offense
2. When offended, not to respond in kind
3. Not to return tit for tat, but to remain calm
4. To offer to suffer injustice
5. To offer to suffer an even greater injustice than your opponent is doing
6. Not to hate the one who perpetrates these things

7. To love the one who harms you
8. Generously to do good deeds for your opponent
9. To pray to God for your adversary.[233]

And we really need to be ready to love in this way. St. Paul issues a warning:

> But understand this, that in the last days there will come times of stress. For men will be lovers of self, lovers of money, proud, arrogant, abusive, disobedient to their parents, ungrateful, unholy, inhuman, implacable, slanderers, profligates, fierce, haters of good, treacherous, reckless, swollen with conceit, lovers of pleasure rather than lovers of God, holding the form of religion but denying the power of it. (2 Timothy 3:1–5)

I think the following words of the Lord from the Gospel of Matthew may be the single most terrifying line in all of the Gospels: "And because wickedness is multiplied, most men's love will grow cold" (Matthew 24:12).

But not ours! Because in our wickedness we have begged for a share in paradise, as did the good thief hanging on his cross next to Jesus Christ. Love will always be what even the most depraved and evil-steeped human heart desires deep down, for *we are made for love*. No matter how much the world may persecute us, we, united with the Crucified, will respond by offering them the paradise Christ gives us.

The indecency and corruption we face nowadays call for a more radical living out of charity. For charity, notes the contemporary Catholic philosopher Fabrice Hadjadj, "demands closeness, to the point of boxing."[234]

And we *can* carry out such charity, as long as we devote ourselves to praying with the certainty of St. Catherine of Siena:

> Eternal Goodness,
> you want me to gaze into you
> and see that you love me,
> to see that you love me gratuitously,
> so that I may love everyone
> with the very same love.
> You want me, then,
> to love and serve my neighbors gratuitously,
> by helping them
> spiritually and materially
> as much as I can,
> without any expectation of selfish profit or pleasure.
> Nor do you want me to hold back
> because of their ingratitude or persecution,
> or for any abuse I may suffer from them.
> What then shall I do
> to come to such a vision?
> I shall strip myself
> of my stinking garment,
> and by the light of my holy faith
> I shall contemplate myself in you.
> And I shall clothe myself in your eternal will.[235]

Notes

1. Quoted at http://www.ncregister.com/site/article/he-fed-us-with-his-words.

2. Quoted at http://archive.thetablet.co.uk/article/19th-may-1984/18/living-prayer.

3. Algar Thorold, trans., *The Dialogue of Saint Catherine of Siena* (London: Kegan Paul, Trench, Trubner, 1907), p. 56.

4. Jean Vanier, *From Brokenness to Community* (New York: Paulist, 1992), pp. 26–27.

5. Josef Pieper, *Faith, Hope, Love*, trans. Richard and Clara Winston (San Francisco: Ignatius, 1997), p. 174.

6. Flannery O'Connor, "Good Country People," in *The Complete Stories* (New York: Farrar, Straus and Giroux, 1971), p. 273.

7. O'Connor, p. 289.

8. Jon Garth Murray, "Closing a Chapter, a Missing Atheist's Belongings Are Sold," *New York Times*, January 25, 1999, available at http://www.nytimes.com/1999/01/25/us/closing-a-chapter-a-missing-atheist-s-belongings-are-sold.html?pagewanted=2.

9. Quoted in Ann Rowe Seaman, *America's Most Hated Woman: The Life and Gruesome Death of Madalyn Murray O'Hair* (New York: Continuum, 2005), p. 149.

10. St. Basil, as quoted in Servais Pinckaers, O.P., *The Sources of Christian Ethics*, trans. Sr. Mary Thomas Noble, O.P. (Washington, D.C.: Catholic University of America Press, 1995), p. 31.

11. St. Augustine, Sermon 34, 1–3, 5–6: CCL 42, 424–426, as quoted in *Office of Readings* for Tuesday, Easter Week 3.

12. *Jesus of Nazareth: From the Baptism in the Jordan to the Transfiguration*, trans. Adrian J. Walker (New York: Doubleday, 2007), p. 279.

13. See St. Augustine, *Confessions*, bk. 1.

14. Luigi Giussani, *At the Origin of the Christian Claim*, trans. Viviane Hewitt (Montreal: McGill-Queen's University Press, 1998), p. 22.

15. Pope Benedict XVI, *Spe Salvi*, 26–27, http://www.vatican.va/holy_father/benedict_xvi/encyclicals/documents/hf_ben-xvi_enc_20071130_spe-salvi_en.html.

16. Julián Carrón, *What Good Does It Do a Man to Gain the Whole World, If He Then Loses Himself? Spiritual Exercises of the University Students of Communion and Liberation*, trans. Edo Moerlin and Sheila Beatty (Milan, Italy: Traces, 2006), pp. 38–39.

17. St. Francis de Sales, *Treatise on the Love of God*, trans. Dom Henry Benedict Mackey, O.S.B. (Rockford, Ill.: Tan, 1997), p. 83. I am indebted to Fr. Ezra Sullivan, O.P., for recommending this work to me.

18. *Spe Salvi*, 35.

19. *Spe Salvi*, 3.

20. Quoted in Joseph Cardinal Ratzinger, *The God of Jesus Christ: Meditations on the Triune God*, trans. Brian McNeil (San Francisco: Ignatius, 2008), p. 16.

21. Joseph Cardinal Ratzinger, *Principles of Catholic Theology*, trans. Sr. Mary Frances McCarthy, S.N.D. (San Francisco: Ignatius, 1987), pp. 52, 53.

22. Bede Jarrett, O.P., *Classic Catholic Meditations* (Manchester, N.H.: Sophia Institute, 2004), pp. 103, 105.

23. Mark Frost and David Lynch, *Twin Peaks*, series 2, episode 20, 1991.

24. See John T. Cacioppo and William Patrick, *Loneliness: Human Nature and the Need for Social Connection* (New York: Norton, 2008), p. 5.

25. Cacioppo and Patrick, p. 6.

26. Cacioppo and Patrick, pp. 7–8.

27. Cacioppo and Patrick, pp. 7–8.

28. Adapted from Dorothy Day, *The Long Loneliness: The Autobiography of the Legendary Catholic Social Activist* (San Francisco: Harper, 1997), p. 286.

29. Cardinal Joseph Ratzinger, *Introduction to Christianity*, trans. J.R. Foster (San Francisco: Ignatius, 2004), p. 298.

30. Ratzinger, *Introduction to Christianity*, p. 300.

31. Catherine de Hueck Doherty, *Faith*, ed. Patricia Lawton (Combermere, Ont.: Madonna House, 1997), pp. 34, 35.

32. Maurice Zundel, *With God in Our Daily Life*, trans. Florestine Audette, R.J.M. (Sherbrooke, Q.C.: Pauline, 1993), p. 69.

33. Cardinal Joseph Ratzinger, *A Turning Point For Europe?* trans. Brian McNeil, C.R.V. (San Francisco: Ignatius, 1994), pp. 175–177.

34. Hans Urs von Balthasar, as quoted at www.patheos.com.

35. St. Gregory of Narek, as cited in Bernard Bro, O.P., *The Rediscovery of Prayer*, trans. John Morriss (Canfield, Ohio: Alba, 1966), pp. 192–193.

36. Madeleine Delbrêl, in "Humor—an Integral Part of Loving" and "Long Live Freedom" from *The Joy of Believing*, trans. D. Ralph Wright (Sherbrooke, Q.C.: Pauline, 1993), pp. 75, 91.

37. Available at http://www.crossroadsnyc.com/files/Fatherhoodtranscript.pdf.

38. Ronald Harwood, *The Dresser*, as quoted in Michael Earley and Philippa Keil, eds., *Solo! The Best Monologues of the 80's (Men)* (New York: Applause, 1987), p. 52.

39. Tennessee Williams, *A Streetcar Named Desire*, scenes 6, 11.

40. St. Thomas Aquinas, *Summa Theologica* I, q. 20, a. 1.

41. St. Thomas Aquinas, *Summa Theologica* I, q. 28, a. 6.

42. St. Thomas Aquinas, *Summa Theologica* I, q. 20, a. 1.

43. Cesare Pavese, *Il mestiere di vivere* ("This Business of Living") (Turin, Italy: Einaudi, 1952), p. 190, as quoted in Fr. Julián Carrón, "Beyond Optimism, Hope," *Traces*, no. 2 (February 1, 2009).

44. Pope Benedict XVI, *Deus Caritas Est*, 18, 17.

45. St. Thomas Aquinas, *Summa Theologica* II-II, q. 179, a.1.

46. Julian of Norwich, *Showings*, trans. Edmund Colledge, O.S.A., and James Walsh, S.J. (Mahwah, N.J.: Paulist, 1978), p. 342.

47. Catherine of Siena, *The Dialogue*, trans. Suzanne Noffke (Mahwah, N.J.: Paulist, 1980), p. 143.

48. *Story of a Soul: The Autobiography of St. Thérèse of Lisieux*, trans. John Clarke, O.C.D. (Washington, D.C.: ICS, 1976), p. 159.

49. *Letters of St. Thérèse of Lisieux, Volume II*, trans. John Clarke, O.C.D. (Washington, D.C.: ICS, 1988), pp. 1093–1094, 1121–1122.

50. *Story of a Soul*, p. 189.

51. St. Leo the Great, Christmas sermon, *Sermon 6 in Nativitate Domini*, 2–3, 5: *PL* 54, 213–216, as excerpted at the Crossroads Initiative, www.crossroadsinitiative.com.

52. Common Preface IV, www.liturgies.net.

53. Eucharistic Prayer I, http://www.usccb.org/prayer-and-worship/the-mass/the-eucharistic_prayer.cfm.

54. Eucharistic Prayer III, www.usccb.org.

55. St. Catherine of Siena, *The Dialogue*, in Mary O'Driscoll, ed., *Catherine of Siena: Passion for the Truth, Compassion for Humanity* (Hyde Park, N.Y.: New City, 2005), p. 122.

56. *Story of a Soul*, p. 256.

57. Delbrêl, p. 75.

58. St. Columban, from *Office of Readings*, Tuesday, Week 4, http://divineoffice.org.

59. Dom Aelred Graham, *The Love of God: An Essay in Analysis* (London: Longmans, Green, 1939), pp. 49–50.

60. St. John Chrysostom, From a homily on the Second letter to the Corinthians, homily 13, 1–2: PG 61, 491–492, as excerpted in *Office of Readings*, Saturday, week 16, www.liturgies.net.

61. See http://www.ccel.org/ccel/schaff/npnf209.iii.iv.iv.xvii.html.

62. John Paul II, *Crossing the Threshold of Hope*, ed. Vittorio Messori (New York: Alfred A. Knopf, 1994), p. 228.

63. Greg Bellow, *Saul Bellow's Heart: A Son's Memoir* (New York: Bloomsbury, 2013), p. 72.

64. Cardinal Joseph Ratzinger, *Co-Workers of the Truth*, trans. Sr. Mary Frances McCarthy, S.N.D., and Rev. Lothar Krauth (San Francisco: Ignatius, 1992), pp. 97–98.

65. J.R.R. Tolkien, Letter 45, June 9, 1941, available at http://glim.ru.

66. Julián Carrón, *Christ in His Beauty Draws Me to Him: Exercises of the Fraternity of Community and Liberation* (Milan, Italy: Comunione e Liberazione, 2007), pp. 15–16.

67. Joseph Campbell with Bill Moyers, *The Power of Myth* (New York: Random House, 2011), p. 209.

68. Massimo Camisasca, *Fraternity and Mission* newsletter, Rome, June, 2003, p. I.

69. Adrienne Von Speyr, as quoted in Fr. Luigi Giussani, "How a Movement Is Born," *Communion and Liberation* newsletter, Covara, Italy, August 1989, http://english.clonline.org/default.asp?id=560&id_n=14552.

70. Christopher O'Mahony, *St. Thérèse of Lisieux by Those Who Knew Her* (Dublin: Veritas, 1975), p. 250.

71. *Story of a Soul*, pp. 224, 158, 200, 195.

72. Mother speaking to Adam, in Fr. Karol Wojtyla (Pope John Paul II), *Radiation of Fatherhood*, 1964, available at http://www.catholicculture.com/ Radiation_of_Fatherhood.pdf.

73. Prayer of Elizabeth of the Trinity, quoted in *CCC*, 260.

74. St. Thérèse of Lisieux, "A Lily Among Thorns," as quoted in Theodore E. James, ed., *The Heart of Catholicism: Essential Writings of the Church From St. Paul to John Paul II* (Huntington, Ind.: Our Sunday Visitor, 1997), p. 548.

75. Msgr. Luigi Giussani, *You or About Friendship: Exercises of the Fraternity of Communion and Liberation* (Milan, Italy: Fraternita di Comunione e Liberazione, 1997), p. 31.

76. Joseph Ratzinger, *Principles of Catholic Theology*, trans. Sr. Mary Frances McCarthy, S.N.D. (San Francisco: Ignatius, 1987), pp. 79–80.

77. Aelred of Rievaulx, *Spiritual Friendship*, trans. Sr. Mary Eugenia Laker, S.S.N.D. (Kalamazoo, Mich.: Cistercian, 1977), pp. 72–73.

78. St. Thomas Aquinas, *Commentary on the Gospel of John*, John 17, lecture 5, no. 2250, http://dhspriory.org/thomas/SSJohn.htm.

79. C.S. Lewis, *The Problem of Pain* (San Francisco: HarperCollins, 1996), pp. 150, 153.

80. St. Gregory the Great, as quoted in *The Sermons and Conferences of John Tauler*, trans. Very Rev. Walter Elliott (Washington, D.C.: Apostolic Mission House, 1910), p. 64.

81. Saul Bellow, *Henderson the Rain King* (New York: Penguin, 1987), p. 24.

82. Blessed Simon Fidati of Cascia, as quoted in *A Word in Season, Readings for the Liturgy of the Hours*, vol. 8 (Villanova: Augustinian, 1999), pp. 158–159.

83. Congregation for Divine Worship and the Discipline of the Sacraments, *Directory on Popular Piety and the Liturgy*, December 2001, no. 166, http://www.vatican.va/roman_curia/congregations/ccdds/documents/ rc_con_ccdds_doc_20020513_vers-direttorio_en.html.

84. Hans Urs Von Balthasar, *Heart of the World*, trans. Erasmo Leiva (San Francisco: Ignatius, 1979), pp. 32, 33.

85. Pope Benedict XVI, homily Solemnity of the Sacred Heart of Jesus, Opening of the Year For Priests on the 150th Anniversary of the Death of Saint John Mary Vianney, June 19, 2009, http://www.vatican.va/holy_father/benedict_xvi/letters/2009/documents/ hf_ben-xvi_let_20090616_anno-sacerdotale_en.html.

86. *The Poetry of Saint Thérèse of Lisieux*, trans. Donald Kinney, O.C.D. (Washington, D.C.: ICS, 1996), pp. 119–120.

87. St. Thomas Aquinas, *Summa Contra Gentiles*, bk. 4, chap. 21, http://dhspriory.org/thomas/ContraGentiles1.htm#21.

88. Msgr. Robert Hugh Benson, *The Friendship of Christ* (Westminster, Md.: Newman, 1955), p. 17.

89. Walter Hilton, *The Scale of Perfection*, trans. Dom Gerard Sitwell, O.S.B. (Westminster, Md.: Newman, 1953), pp. 293–294.

90. *Fraternity and Mission* (Newsletter of the Priestly Fraternity of the Missionaries of St. Charles Borromeo) (Rome: Fraternity of the Missionaries of St. Charles Borromeo, 2003), p. 1.
91. St. Thomas Aquinas, *Summa Contra Gentiles,* trans. English Dominican Fathers (New York: Benziger, 1954), chap. 21, p. 92, http://www.archive.org/stream/summacontragenti02thomuoft/summacontragenti02thomuoft_djvu.txt.
92. *Thoughts and Sayings of Saint Margaret Mary,* trans. Sisters of the Visitation of Partridge Green (Rockford, Ill.: Tan, 1986), pp. 34–37; *The Letters of St. Margaret Mary Alacoque,* trans. Fr. Clarence A. Herbst, S.J. (Rockford, Ill.: Tan, 1997), pp. 73–74.
93. *The Spiritual Direction of Saint Claude de le Colombière,* trans. Mother M. Philip, I.B.V.M. (San Francisco: Ignatius, 1998), p. 24.
94. Quoted at http://www.ascjus.org/who-we-are/sharing-our-charism/sacred-heart-spirituality/saints/index.aspx.
95. Available at http://www.traces-cl.com/feb02/ptn.html.
96. Luigi Giussani, *Why the Church?* (Montreal: McGill-Queen, 2001), pp. 73, 74, 75.
97. Pope Benedict XVI, *Jesus of Nazareth: Holy Week, From the Entrance Into Jerusalem to the Resurrection* (San Francisco: Ignatius, 2011), p. 96.
98. *Christ Is Everything in Everyone,* Exercises of the Fraternity of Communion and Liberation, trans. Patrick Stevenson (Milan: Fraternita di Comunion e Liberazione, 1999), pp. 47, 29, Luigi Giussani, *The Religious Sense,* trans. John Zucchi (Montreal: McGill-Queen, 1997), p. 106.
99. Letter from Vincent van Gogh to Theo van Gogh, July 1980, http://www.webexhibits.org/vangogh/letter/8/133.htm.
100. Quoted at Dan Lynch Apostolates, "St. Isaac Jogues," http://jkmi.wsiefusion.net/saints-isaac-jogues-rene-goupil-and-jean-de-la-lande.
101. See Pseudo-Hugh of St. Victor, Explanation of the Rule of St. Augustine, 5–6, http://studyandliturgy.wordpress.com.
102. Luigi Giussani, *The Risk of Education,* trans. Rosanna M. Giammanco Frongia (New York: Crossroad, 2001), p. 74.
103. Augustin Guillerand, *Where Silence Is Praise,* trans. a Carthusian monk of Parkminster (London: Darton, Longman & Todd, 1960), pp. 43–44.
104. Xavier Beauvois, *Of Gods and Men* (Sony, 2011).
105. *The Spiritual Direction of Saint Claude de la Colombière,* p. 133.
106. Fr. Pedro Arrupe, S.J. (+1991), 28th Superior General of the Society of Jesus, as quoted at http://www.ignatianspirituality.com/ignatian-prayer/prayers-by-st-ignatius-and-others/fall-in-love/.
107. Benson, p. ix.
108. Charles de Foucauld, Prayer of Abandonment, as quoted at http://www.crossroadsinitiative.com/library_article/212/Prayer_of_Abandonment__Charles_de_Foucauld.html.
109. Marthe Robin, as quoted in Raymond Peyret, *The Cross and the Joy,* trans. Clare W. Faulhaber (Staten Island, N.Y.: Alba, 1983), pp. 86–87.
110. Audrey Assad and Sharon Hart, "Show Me," River Oaks Music, 2010.

111.   St. Faustina Kowalska, *Diary*, #300, as quoted at http://thedivinemercy.org/
       library/faq/clergyanswers.php?newsID=93.

112.   Pope John Paul II, *Dives in Misericordia*, Encyclical on Divine
       Mercy, November 30, 1980, 6, 7. Available at http://www.
       vatican.va/holy_father/john_paul_ii/encyclicals/documents/
       hf_jp-ii_enc_30111980_dives-in-misericordia_en.html.

113.   Jacques Fesch, as quoted in Leo Knowles, *Modern Heroes of the Church*
       (Huntington, Ind.: Our Sunday Visitor, 2003), p. 164.

114.   Cardinal Bergoglio, talk at the Buenos Aires International Book Fair,
       presenting the Spanish edition of *L'attrattiva Gesù* [The Attraction That Is
       Jesus], April 27, 2001, as quoted in Silvina Primat, "The Attraction of the
       Cardinal," www.traces-cl.com.

115.   St. Thomas Aquinas, *Summa Theologica* I, q. 21, a. 4.

116.   Giussani, *The Risk of Education*, pp. 40–41.

117.   Eben Alexander, *Proof of Heaven: A Neurosurgeon's Journey into the
       Afterlife* (New York: Simon and Schuster, 2012), p. 40.

118.   Julián Carrón, *The Destiny of Man*, Exercises of the Fraternity of
       Communion and Liberation, trans. Susan Scott and Don Edo Morlin
       Visconti (Milan, Italy: Fraternita di Comunione e Liberazione, 2004), p. 25.

119.   Julián Carrón, *You Live for Love of Something Happening Now*, Exercises
       of the Fraternity of Communion and Liberation, trans. Patrick Stevenson
       (Milan, Italy: Fraternita di Comunione e Liberazione, 2006), p. 47.

120.   St. Thomas Aquinas, *Commentary on the Gospel of John Books 1–5*, trans.
       Fabian Larcher, O.P., and James A. Weisheipl, O.P. (Washington, D.C.:
       Catholic University of America Press, 2010), no. 2619, p. 296.

121.   Jacques Benigne Bossuet, *Devotion to the Blessed Virgin Mary: Being
       the Substance of All the Sermons for Mary's Feasts Throughout the Year*
       (London: Longmans, Green, 1899), pp. 42, 46.

122.   Joseph Holzner, *Paul of Tarsus* (London: Scepter, 2002), pp. 38, 39.

123.   Pope Benedict XVI, General Audience November 8, 2006, http://
       www.vatican.va/holy_father/benedict_xvi/audiences/2006/documents/
       hf_ben-xvi_aud_20061108_en.html.

124.   Pope Benedict XVI, *Deus Caritas Est*, Encyclical on Christian Love,
       December 25, 2005, 1, http://www.vatican.va/holy_father/benedict_xvi/
       encyclicals/documents/hf_ben-xvi_enc_20051225_deus-caritas-est_en.html.

125.   St. Anselm, Meditation IV, "Concerning the Redemption of Mankind"
       in *Devotions of St. Anselm Archbishop of Canterbury*. Christian Classics
       Ethereal Library, p. 119, available at www.ccel.org.http://www.ccel.org/ccel/
       anselm/devotions.iii.vi.html.

126.   Holzner, p. 77.

127.   St. John Chrysostom, homily preached around A.D. 400 in praise of St. Paul
       (*Hom. 2 de laudibus sancti Pauli*: PG 50, 477–480), used in the Roman
       Office of Readings for the Feast of the Conversion of Saint Paul on January
       25, available at http://www.crossroadsinitiative.com/library_article/440/
       In_Praise_of_St._Paul__John_Chrysostom.html.

128. St. Fulgentius of Ruspe, sermon for the feast of St. Stephen (Sermon 3, 1–3, 5–6: CCL 91A, 905–909), circa A.D. 500, http://www.crossroadsinitiative. com/library_article/841/Feast_of_St_Stephen__Protomartyr_Fulgentius_of_ Ruspe.html.

129. St. Diadochus of Photiki, "On Spiritual Knowledge and Discrimination," no. 27, in St. Nikodimos of the Holy Mountain and St. Markarios of Corinth, *The Philokalia, Volume 1: The Complete Text*, trans. J.E.H. Palmer, Philip Sherrard, and Kallistos Ware (London: Faber and Faber, 1979), p. 260.

130. St. Catherine of Siena, in Matthew Levering, ed., *On Prayer and Contemplation: Classic and Contemporary Texts* (Lanham, Md.: Rowman and Littlefield, 2005), p. 83.

131. Catherine of Siena, *The Dialogue*, p. 270.

132. Victor Hugo, *Les Miserables*, chap. 12, available at http://www.online-litera-ture.com/victor_hugo/les_miserables/26/.

133. Paul Claudel, *I Believe in God: A Meditation on the Apostles' Creed*, ed. Agnes du Sarment, trans. Helen Weaver (New York: Holt, Rinehart, and Winston, 1963), pp. 31, 32.

134. St. Alphonsus Liguori, "On the Love of Christ," as quoted at http://www. crossroadsinitiative.com/library_article/695/On_the_Love_of_Christ_St_ Alphonsus_Liguori.html.

135. From the teachings of Saint Dorotheus, abbot, Doctrine 13, *De accusatione sui ipsius*, 1–3, available at http://dominicanidaho.org/meditation_dorotheus. html.

136. George Bernanos, "Agenda," as quoted in Hans Urs von Balthasar, *Bernanos: An Ecclesial Existence* (San Francisco: Ignatius, 1996).

137. Maria Rilke, "Ich bette wieder, du Erlauchter," in Anita Barrows and Joanna Macy, trans., *Rilke's Book of Hours: Love Poems to God* (New York: Riverhead, 2005), p. 98.

138. Letter from St. Thérèse to Sr. Marie of the Sacred Heart, in John Clarke, O.C.D., trans., *Letters of St. Thérèse of Lisieux Volume II, 1890–1897* (Washington, D.C.: ICS, 1988), p. 999.

139. Christopher O'Mahony, *St. Thérèse of Lisieux by Those Who Knew Her* (Dublin: Veritas, 1975), p. 250.

140. *Story of a Soul*, pp. 224, 258, 200, 195.

141. Pope Benedict XVI, *Credo for Today: What Christians Believe*, trans. Henry Taylor (San Francisco: Ignatius, 2009), p. 126.

142. St. Thérèse of Lisieux, *Letters 1890–1897*, p. 795.

143. St. Thérèse of Lisieux, as quoted in Francis Broome, C.S.P., trans., *The Little Way for Every Day: Thoughts from Thérèse of Lisieux* (Mahwah, N.J.: Paulist, 2006), p. 21.

144. St. Augustine, "My Sacrifice Is a Contrite Spirit," excerpts from sermon on Psalm 51, Sermon 19, 2–3, CCL: 41, 252–254, available at www.crossroad-sinitiative.com.

145. Luigi Giussani, *You Live for Love of Something Happening Now*, p. 20.

146. Giussani, *Why the Church?*, p. 111.

147.   This prayer was found on the body of Lieutenant André Zirnheld, killed in action in Libya in July 1942, during a raid behind enemy lines. A college philosophy professor before the war, this aspirant to the priesthood served in one of the very first companies of the famed British S.A.S. The National Institute for the Renewal of the Priesthood, http://www.jknirp.com/zirn.htm.

148.   Mother Teresa of Calcutta, as quoted in "Suffering in Serving Others," http://saintquotes.blogspot.com/2009/06/suffering-through-course-of-ones-own.html.

149.   Joseph Ratzinger, *God and the World: Believing and Living in Our Time* (San Francisco: Ignatius, 2002), p. 332.

150.   *Spe Salvi*, 38.

151.   Gertrude von Le Fort, "A Prayer for People Who Want to Believe in God," http://prayers4reparation.wordpress.com.

152.   Fr. Dominique Barthelemy, O.P., *God and His Image: An Outline of Biblical Theology*, trans. Dom Aldhelm Dean (San Francisco: Ignatius, 2007), p. 55.

153.   Léon Bloy, as quoted in Richard Leonard, S.J., *Movies That Matter: Reading Film through the Lens of Faith* (Chicago: Loyola, 2006), p. 14.

154.   Pope John Paul II, *Salvifici Doloris*, Apostolic Letter on the Christian Meaning of Human Suffering, February 11, 1984, 1, 22, http://www.vatican.va/holy_father/john_paul_ii/apost_letters/documents/hf_jp-ii_apl_11021984_salvifici-doloris_en.html.

155.   Fr. Julián Carrón, *Friends, That Is, Witnesses*, Communion and Liberation Responsibles' International Assembly, trans. Patrick Stevenson (Milan, Italy: Traces, 2007), p. 19.

156.   Scott O'Grady, "It Took A Mighty Big Jolt to Open My Eyes," *Parade*, October 19, 1995.

157.   Interview with Msgr. Lorenzo Albacete, *Religion and Ethics Newsweekly*, November 15, 2002.

158.   Viktor E. Frankl, *Man's Search for Meaning*, trans. Ilse Lasch (Boston: Beacon, 2006), pp. 113, 115, 119, 148.

159.   Louis Lavelle, *The Dilemma of Narcissus*, trans. W.T. Gairdner (Burdett: Larson, 1993), pp. 102, 103, 104, 105.

160.   Ron Block, "There Is a Reason." Used by permission of Hal Leonard.

161.   Michael Bellmore, "Lapsed Catholic Has a Confession to Make," *New Haven Register*, December 23, 2012.

162.   Jenny Hubbard, "A Mother's Faith," http://cajetano.blogspot.com/2013/03/a-mothers-faith.html.

163.   St. Rose of Lima, "Beauty of Grace," used for Office of Readings on her feast day, August 23, excerpted from http://www.crossroadsinitiative.com/library_article/712/Beauty_of_Divine_Grace_St_Rose_of_Lima.html.

164.   John Paul II, *Crossing the Threshold of Hope*, p. 66.

165.   Spoken by Anne Vercors in Paul Claudel, *The Tidings Brought to Mary: A Mystery*, trans. Louise Morgan Sill (New Haven, Conn.: Yale University Press, 1956), act 1, scene 1, p. 35.

166.   Cardinal Joseph Ratzinger, *Truth and Tolerance: Christian Belief and World Religions*, trans. Henry Taylor (San Francisco: Ignatius, 2004), pp. 70–71.

167. Don Camillo in Paul Claudel, *The Satin Slipper; or, the Worst Is Not the Surest,* trans. Fr. John O'Connor (New York: Sheed & Ward, 1947), Third Day, scene 10, p. 97.

168. Fr. Simon Tugwell, as quoted in Dr. David Bissonnette, "Finding Healing in the Divine. True Love" Catholic Online, September 27, 2010, available at http://www.catholic.org/hf/faith/story.php?id=38434&wf=rsscol.

169. Bernanos, as quoted in von Balthasar , *Bernanos: An Ecclesial Existence* (San Francisco: Ignatius, 1996).

170. Pope Benedict XVI, *Spe Salvi,* 38.

171. Jacques Fesch, as quoted in Jim Dudley, "Murderer Jacques Fesch," August 20, 2009, http://www.examiner.com/article/murderer-jacques-fesch.

172. Pope John Paul II, *Dives in Misericordia,* 8.

173. Cardinal Joseph Ratzinger and Peter Seewald, *God and the World: Believing and Living in Our Time* (San Francisco: Ignatius, 2002), p. 323.

174. Pope Benedict XVI, *Spe Salvi,* 37.

175. Paul Claudel, quoted in Daniel Lanahan, *When God Says No: The Mystery of Suffering and the Dynamics of Prayer* (New York: Lantern, 2001), p. 71.

176. Pope Benedict XVI, *Credo for Today,* p. 75.

177. Fr. Servais Pinckaers, *The Sources of Christian Ethics,* trans. Sr. Mary Thomas Noble (Washington, D.C.: Catholic University of America Press, 1995), pp. 24, 25.

178. Pope John Paul II, *Salvifici Doloris,* 26.

179. *Mother Teresa: Come Be My Light,* ed. Brian Kolodiejchuk, M.C. (New York: Doubleday, 2007), pp. 186–187.

180. *Story of a Soul,* p. 152.

181. St. Thérèse of Lisieux, Letter 76, January 7, 1889, as quoted in Francois Jamart, *Complete Spiritual Doctrine of St. Thérèse of Lisieux,* trans. Rev. Walther Van de Putte, C.S.SP. (Staten Island, N.Y.: Alba House, 1961), p. 214.

182. Ratzinger, *God and the World,* p. 322.

183. St. Gregory Nazianzen, homily, used in the Divine Office on Saturday the fifth week of Lent.

184. *The Collected Works of St. Teresa of Ávila, Volume One,* trans. Kieran Kavanaugh, O.C.D. and Otilio Rodriguez, O.C.D. (Washington, D.C.: ICS, 1987), pp. 220–221.

185. Catherine of Siena, *The Dialogue,* p. 33.

186. Thomas à Kempis, *The Imitation of Christ* (Milwaukee: Bruce, 1949), bk. 3, chap. 30; bk. 2, chap. 12; bk. 3, chap. 19, available at http://www.ccel.org/ccel/kempis/imitation.toc.html.

187. Pope John Paul II, *Salvifici Doloris,* 18.

188. David Gelernter, as quoted in Jocelyn McClurg, "After the Unabomber: Yale Professor Writes of the Explosion That Could Have Destroyed Him," *The Courant,* September 13, 1997, available at http://articles.courant.com/1997-09-13/features/9709130048_1_yale-computer-science-professor-blood-pressure-hand.

189. David Gelernter, as quoted in Scott Holleran, "Drawing Life: Unabomber Target Ponders Life Before, After Attack," available at http://www.scottholleran.com/old/books/drawing-life.htm.

190. Caryll Houselander, "Sharing Christ's Sufferings Is the Most Effective of All Acts of Love," as quoted at http://prayers4reparation.wordpress.com.

191. Catherine de Hueck Doherty, *Fragments of My Life: A Memoir* (Combermere, Ont.: Madonna House, 1996), pp. 115–116.

192. Jacques Maritain, *Raïssa's Journal* (Petersham, Mass.: St. Bede's, 1974), p. 43.

193. *Story of a Soul*, pp. 237, 241.

194. Cardinal Joseph Ratzinger, *The Spirit of the Liturgy* (San Francisco: Ignatius, 2000), p. 33.

195. Cardinal Joseph Ratzinger, *Introduction to Christianity* (San Francisco: Ignatius, 2004), p. 215.

196. Pope Benedict XVI, Homily for Twentieth World Youth Day Eucharistic Celebration, August 21, 2005, http://www.vatican.va/holy_father/benedict_xvi/homilies/2005/documents/hf_ben-xvi_hom_20050821_20th-world-youth-day_en.html.

197. Pope Benedict XVI, Homily, August 21, 2005.

198. Antonin Sertillanges, O.P., *Spirituality*, trans. Dominican Nuns, Corpus Christi Monastery (New York: McMullen, 1954), p. 176.

199. Henry Suso, *The Exemplar, with Two German Sermons,* trans. Frank Tobin (New York: Paulist, 1989), p. 360.

200. Richard Rolle, "The Name of Jesus Makes a Contemplative Man," as quoted by Dom Mark Daniel Kirby, http://vultus.stblogs.org/index.php/2012/01/the-name-of-jesus-makes-a-cont/.

201. St. Thérèse of Lisieux, *The Little Way for Every Day: Thoughts from Thérèse of Lisieux*, trans. Fr. Francis Broome (Mahwah, N.J.: Paulist, 2006), entry for February 9.

202. St. Francis de Sales, *Introduction to the Devout Life*, trans. John K. Ryan (Garden City, N.J.: Image, 1950), pp. 249, 88–89.

203. Abbé Berlioux, *Month of the Sacred Heart: Or Practical Meditations for Each Day of the Month of June*, trans. Laetitia Selwyn Oliver (Dublin: M.H. Gill and Son, 1885), pp. 80–81.

204. St. Thérèse of Lisieux, *Story of a Soul,* as quoted in Pope Benedict XVI, *Verbum Domini*, Post-Synodal Exhortation on the Word of God in the Life and Mission of the Church, September 30, 2010, 48, http://www.vatican.va/holy_father/benedict_xvi/apost_exhortations/documents/hf_ben-xvi_exh_20100930_verbum-domini_en.html.

205. Ardo Smaragdus, *Comm. In Reg. S. Benedicti*, 4,56 (PL 102, 784), as quoted in Rev. Randy Soto, *Lectio Divina: Praying With the Word of God,* p. 2.

206. Pope Benedict XVI, *Verbum Domini*, 51.

207. Myles Connolly, *Mr. Blue* (Chicago: Loyola, 2005), pp. 80–84.

208. Excerpt from St. Thomas Aquinas, "Prayer for Leading a Holy Life," as quoted at http://www.catholicity.com/prayer/prayer-for-leading-a-holy-life.html.

209. Rose Hawthorne, as quoted in Diana Culbertson, O.P., ed., *Rose Hawthorne Lathrop* (Mahwah, N.J.: Paulist, 1993), pp. 195–196.
210. Charles Péguy, as quoted in Adam Michnik, *The Church and the Left*, ed. and trans. David Ost (Chicago: University of Chicago Press, 1993), p. 195.
211. St. John of the Cross, as quoted in Brendan Leahy, *Believe in Love: The Life, Ministry and Teachings of John Paul II* (Hyde Park, N.Y.: New City, 2011), p. 148.
212. Pope Benedict XVI, *Deus Caritas Est,* 7.
213. *Story of a Soul*, pp. 220, 221.
214. Quoted at http://archive.thetablet.co.uk/article/19th-may-1984/18/living-prayer.
215. *The Cloud of Unknowing*, as quoted in Susan Muto, *Blessings that Make Us Be: A Formative Approach to Living the Beatitudes* (Petersham, Mass.: St. Bede's, 1982), p. 22.
216. Á la Pope Benedict XVI, in *Jesus of Nazareth*, p. 233.
217. Pope Benedict XVI, *Deus Caritas Est,* 17.
218. George Bernanos, *Diary of a Country Priest* (New York: De Capo, 2002), pp. 163, 165.
219. Fr. Walter Hilton, *The Scale of Perfection,* as quoted at http://hcikfs.blogspot.com/2011_02_01_archive.html.
220. Enzo Piccinini, *Ideal Thinks He Thou Alone Are True* (Milan: Traces, 1999), p. 16.
221. Seneca, as quoted in Luigi Giussani, *Is It Possible to Live This Way: An Unusual Approach to Christian Existence* (Montreal: McGill-Queen, 2009), p. 27.
222. Dorothy Day, as quoted at http://www.goodreads.com/quotes/215500-i-really-only-love-god-as-much-as-i-love.
223. Dorothy Day, *The Long Loneliness: The Autobiography of the Legendary Catholic Social Activist* (San Francisco: Harper, 1997), p. 285.
224. Pope Benedict XVI, *Deus Caritas Est,*18.
225. St. Gregory the Great, as quoted in St. Thomas Aquinas, *Commentary on the Gospel of John Chapters 13–21*, trans. Fabian Larcher, O.P., and James A. Weisheipl, O.P. (Washington, D.C.: American Catholic University Press, 2010), p. 82.
226. Pope Benedict XVI, *Deus Caritas Est,* 16, 18.
227. Louis Lavelle, *The Dilemma of Narcissus,* trans. W.T. Gairdner (Burdett, N.Y.: Larson, 1993), pp. 216, 217.
228. Pope John XXIII, *Days of Devotion,* trans. John P. Donnelly (New York: Penguin, 1996), pp. 27–28.
229. St. Thomas Aquinas, *Summa Theologica* II-II, q. 25, a. 1.
230. Msgr. Luigi Giussani, "The Meaning of Charitable Work," available at http://communio.stblogs.org/Meaning%20of%20Charitable%20Work.pdf.
231. Fr. Reginald Garrigou-Lagrange, "The Purification of the Soul in Beginners," from a course given for over twenty years at the Angelicum in Rome, www.christianperfection.info.
232. Elie Wiesel, as quoted in Jeremy Dick, *Language of the Spirit: 99 Devotionals* (Bloomington, Ind.: AuthorHouse, 2006), p. 78.

233.   St. John Chrysostom, as cited in *The Great Commentary of Cornelius a Lapide,* vol. 1, trans. Thomas W. Mossman (Fitzwilliam, N.H.: Loreto, 2008), pp. 283–284.

234.   Fabrice Hadjadj, as quoted in Luca Doninelli, "Close-up at the Heart of Our Need: The Peripheries of Existence, Going out of Ourselves in Order to Understand Who We Are," *Traces,* no. 5, May 1, 2013.

235.   *The Prayers of Catherine of Siena, 2nd Edition,* trans. Suzanne Noffke, O.P. (San Jose, Calif.: Authors Choice, 2001), p. 114.